Assemblies Round the Year

Beverley Birch

with music chosen by Margaret Hope-Brown
and illustrations by Jenny Williams

Ward Lock Educational

WARD LOCK EDUCATIONAL CO., LTD.
BIC LING KEE HOUSE
1 CHRISTOPHER ROAD
EAST GRINSTEAD
SUSSEX RH19 3BT
UNITED KINGDOM

A MEMBER OF THE LING KEE GROUP
HONG KONG · SINGAPORE · LONDON · NEW YORK

Text © Beverley Birch

First published – 1985
Reprinted – 1986, 1989, 1991, 1993, 1996

ISBN 0-7062-4469-9

Printed in Hong Kong

Contents

(The items in italics are songs.)

Foreword

In choosing and writing these assembly readings I have tried to provide a range of subjects: entries which explain how months got their names or which reflect the changing seasons and weather; stories and myths from different parts of the world; notes about sporting achievements; descriptions of historical events which mean something to children and which show how our lives have altered and developed; accounts of great disasters from which positive achievements or changes arose; reminders of the courageous work of individuals to correct injustices, help the sick or make life better for us all; and of course the stories behind many of the major festivals.

Some readings are attached to relevant dates, others are seasonally linked, some could be used at any time of the year. With Scottish schools in mind, I have started the school year in August but the readings for August can, of course, be used by other schools at other times of the year.

I have cross referenced many entries so that, if you don't use them on the days to which they are allocated, you can pick them up on other appropriate days later in the year. Wherever relevant, I have also given references to two other Ward Lock Educational books, *Faiths and Festivals* and *A Musical Calendar of Festivals*, where you will find additional material for many occasions.

Occasionally in the readings I have asked a question of the audience, drawn a moral or spelt out a message but mostly I have deliberately avoided doing this (or providing prayers). It seems to me that this aspect of assembly is a very personal one. Different teachers have different approaches: their own way of interpreting ideas for their particular group of children or involving them and inviting their participation in what is being read. So I hope that you will make these readings very much your own — that you will comment, add, adapt, omit, chop and change. Some of the longer pieces could be split up and used on several days. Some could be followed up in the classroom afterwards. All of them are written and chosen in the hope that they will provide interest and relevance to your assemblies all around the year.

Beverley Birch

Note to readers

To refer you to relevant material, including songs, in other Ward Lock Educational books we have used this symbol ▶

The following abbreviations are used for different books:

MCF : A Musical Calendar of Festivals
F&F : Faiths and Festivals
ECUS : Every Colour Under the Sun
FCYC : Folk Carols for Young Children
BBB : Brown Bread and Butter

Full details of these and other Ward Lock Educational music and assembly books can be found on page 128.

Throughout this book, the terms CE (Common Era) and BCE (Before Common Era) are used when referring to dates instead of the terms AD and BC.

Square brackets [ ] show figures that are correct at the time of publication [1986] but which may have to be altered in subsequent years.

Autumn Term

August

In some years the following festival may fall in August:

Eid ul-Adha (Muslim festival). ▶F&F.

August's name

Imagine this month being called 'The moon when the geese lose their feathers,' or 'The moon when the yellow flowers bloom,' or 'The corn is in the silk moon' or 'The big-ripening moon'. These names were used by the Indian nations of North America, recalling vividly how plants and animals change with the passing seasons of the year. They called their months 'moons', because they measured them by the waxing and waning of the moon.

If we named the months like this, what would you call August?

The word 'August' actually comes from a Roman Emperor, Caesar Augustus. Nearly 2000 years ago, he improved the calendar then used by the Romans. To honour him, one of the months (which was then simply called 'the fifth month'), was renamed 'Augustus'. And so we get our name 'August'.

In fact all the months, from January to December, take their names from those the Ancient Romans used. It is their calendar which is the foundation of the one used in this country nowadays, and it was first brought to Britain when the Romans conquered it.

See also January, February, March, April, May, June, July.

The home of Barbarians

'. . . a thoroughly unattractive place, wet, misty, dull, the home of Barbarians deceitful to a civilised Mediterranean man . . .'

Can you guess which country this is? It is Britain, as it appeared to a writer nearly 2000 years ago!

Six hundred years later, another said '. . . it is therefore inhabited only by the souls of the dead who are ferried thither across the Channel. The climate north of the Roman wall is so pestilential that only serpents can live there.'

This was probably said because the Romans never did succeed in conquering the Picts of the north (in what is now Scotland). The Romans built a great wall to stop the Picts raiding southwards into Roman territory.

Unfamiliar things have always made people nervous, suspicious, or downright afraid. The Romans thought of Britain like this, because it was very different from their own warmer country, and its people lived and behaved in ways which they found difficult to understand.

Then, as now, people were quick to describe a way of life which was unlike the one they knew, as somehow worse, bad, or even dangerous.

Their imaginations ran wild. When, just over 700 years ago Marco Polo travelled overland to the east from Venice, his descriptions of the animals he saw seemed very strange to people in Europe. They imagined the most extraordinary monsters. Marco spoke of enormous four-legged serpents, their mouths huge enough to swallow a man in one gulp. We now know that he was describing a crocodile.

He also talked of a unicorn, very large, not much smaller than an elephant. It was ugly, had a single black horn in the middle of its forehead, and its huge heavy head was always carried sloping to the ground. He was, in fact, describing a rhinoceros. But to those in Europe who had never seen one, it was as fearsome a beast as anything they could possibly imagine.

One hundred years after Marco lived, the book about his travels had been widely read. People knew of the rich, powerful, and civilised countries he had visited in the east, peopled not by monsters, but by men, women and children.

Yet artists still drew people from those lands with no heads, their faces on their chests, one enormous leg and a single foot protruding from their bodies.

Nearly three centuries later, vast areas of the world had been visited by sailors from Europe. At

the same time others, who had never left Europe, still believed that monsters and foul, murderous spirits lurked in the oceans around America and the East. Seamen brought home tales of huge whales, man-eating sharks, dolphins that leapt high above the waves, eels, octopuses, swordfish, giant rays and squid. This was, of course, long before photography had been invented, so unless a traveller could draw what had been seen, people had no idea what it really looked like. They imagined fish the size of mountains which roamed the sea looking for ships to overturn; serpents 100 metres long, which crushed sailing vessels to matchwood with their coils; great winged monsters, with tusks that reached the sky, terrifying horns, flaming breath, eyes 20 metres wide . . . One Swiss artist even illustrated the fruit of a tree which grew ducks!

Although people nowadays may not imagine unfamiliar animals as fire-breathing monsters, or people they have never seen as having their noses in the middle of their stomachs, nevertheless in their own, often quite hidden ways, people can be just as suspicious and a little afraid of things they do not understand. Many, ordinary, harmless things can seem a little threatening if we do not understand the reasons, or cannot share in the mood of an event.

Listen to this description: 'Thousands gathered. All heads turned, anxiously, awaiting the contest in the open space below. The men stood, straight and watchful in their gleaming white.

Then it began. They crouched, ready to spring. Along a streak of brown which sliced across the centre of the space the first one ran, gathered speed, legs pounding, arms drawn towards his chest, and then with all his might he hurled the missile through the air towards his waiting foe — who raised his weapon desperately against the vicious onslaught.

Through the crowd there rose a roar, of mingled pain, surprise and joy. The missile spun away. The defender fled. The crowd now shrieked, as it flew towards the running figure. And then a despairing moan rippled through their ranks; the missile burst pass him and scattered a gate of sticks behind.

Another now prepared to face the onslaught. The white-clad figures moved about the arena. Breathed easy, stretched limbs, raised arms to heaven.

Then it began again. Tensely they crouched. The next victim took his place.'

Would you have known, from this description, that it was only a game of cricket being played?

Can you think of anything which is done in this country, or even in your local community, which would seem very strange to a traveller who had never seen such things before? Is there anything you've heard of in another country, which seems a little frightening to *you*?

Perhaps it seems so only because you really don't know very much about it?

15 August

Not so very long ago, an infection in your body could make you so ill that you would probably die. Doctors had no medicines to treat it, no way of killing germs once they were inside you. There was one *possible* remedy – to cut off the infected limb, and hope to stop the infection spreading. Even a small splinter in your finger might lead to that finger being cut off, for if the germs were allowed to grow in the blood, you could die of blood-poisoning.

It was a Scottish doctor, Alexander Fleming, who changed all this. Like so many doctors and scientists all over the world, he was trying to find a way to destroy the germs which cause disease. As part of his studies he was growing germs on a kind of jelly in small, glass dishes covered with lids. One day in August 1928, in his laboratory at St Mary's Hospital, London, he noticed that one of his germ dishes was uncovered. He went and looked at it a bit more closely. It seemed to have been spoiled, for there was a green mould growing on it, rather like the mould on stale bread. He saw something else. All the germs around that mould had died.

Dr Fleming was a very careful scientist. He never left anything unexplored or unexplained. Could he make other germs die with that mould, he wondered? He transferred some of the mould to other dishes. Again, all the germs around the mould died.

Now he was certain. The mould contained a powerful germ-killer – just the substance he had been searching for throughout his work.

He gave his new discovery the name 'penicillin'. Within sixteen years it would transform the work of doctors throughout the world. It gave them a means of killing many of the germs which cause infection, yet doing so without harming the patient.

Since that time, many other germ killers, or 'anti-biotics' have been found, prompted by the success of Dr Fleming's penicillin.

It was first used on a lot of people in the Second World War. Many wounded soldiers would once have died or had their limbs amputated. But the new penicillin saved them.

It is now used all over the world as a treatment for many different kinds of disease and infection. In this country it is used in every hospital, and by every doctor. Many of you will probably have been given it at least once in your life.

This month, about 60 years from the time he made his first discovery, we should remember this Scottish doctor whose painstaking observation and careful, determined work has benefitted people all over the world, for all time.

See also September 28th.

Steaming down the Clyde

Just over 170 years ago, in 1812, a ship named the *Comet* first took to the waters of the River Clyde in Scotland. A number of people were quite certain she would blow up, for she was one of the first boats with a steam engine to be built and then successfully launched. Until this time, boats were sailing ships – that is driven only by wind power. No ship had any kind of engine.

The *Comet* did not blow up. Instead she spent the next seven years steaming to and fro on the River Clyde between Glasgow and Helensburgh, and then was taken on to more open sea in the Firth of Clyde. Unfortunately, she was wrecked on

August

a rocky shore not long after, but her steam engine was salvaged and is now in the Science Museum in London.

The engine was designed by an engineer named Henry Bell. He was determined to prove that steam could be used to drive a ship, and had approached the Navy with the idea of designing and building such a boat for them. They were convinced that steam could never be used successfully at sea, so they turned him down.

He decided to go ahead and prove it anyway. Having done so with the *Comet*, he went on to build another steamship, the *Margery*, which travelled between London and Gravesend for a while, before becoming the first cross-Channel steamer from Newhaven to Dieppe.

People had been so certain that steamboats would never work, because engineers had been trying to build one for 75 years. One of the earliest attempts was made by two French Army officers on the River Seine in France in 1772. They launched their ship and hoisted the engine into position. But when they returned the next day, the boat had disappeared — sunk to the bottom of the river under the weight of the engine and the bricks on which it rested in the hull of the ship.

All the early engines used were based on the first engine ever invented, by Thomas Newcomen in Britain in 1709. It was very heavy, and not really suited to a vessel that had to stay afloat on water.

James Watt invented an improved kind of steam engine 60 years later, and within fourteen years another Frenchman, the Marquis de Jouffroy had succeeded in launching a boat driven with this kind of engine and having it steam down the river.

But it was another nineteen years before a Scotsman, William Symington, designed the first engine specially for driving a boat. It was made for the tugboat *Charlotte Dundas*, and she successfully towed two barges each weighing 70 tonnes for over 31 kilometres against a headwind. She only took six hours to do it. This would have been quite impossible using a sailing ship.

Unfortunately the Canal company she worked for became worried that the wash of water from her paddles would damage the canal banks, and they stopped running her. Ten years later Henry Bell launched the *Comet*, and steam-driven ships began to appear on canals and rivers throughout Britain.

Yet the Navy remained unimpressed. One reason was that they feared fire breaking out on the wooden boats, for the steam engine was stoked by a furnace. Their fears were not unreasonable — there were several bad fires which destroyed whole ships. It was really only when iron-plated ships began to be built that the Navy changed its mind.

For most people, the new steamboats were hailed as the greatest invention of all time, and pleasure steamers quickly became very popular. Within seven years of the *Comet's* first voyage, a ship fitted with steam engines crossed the Atlantic Ocean. The age of the great luxurious transatlantic steamers was just around the corner.

See also April 9th.

Harvest long ago

Harvest time in this country a hundred years ago was very different from now. Machines now do a great deal of the work; then, a lot more people worked on the land and whole communities were closely tied to it.

Here is a description of harvest-time as it was in the 1880s in Britain. Many of the old methods were still being used, but the first machines were also appearing on the farms. Harvest — a time of hard work for everyone — was followed by the jolliest celebration of the year.

'In the fields where the harvest had begun all was bustle and activity. At that time the mechanical reaper with long, red, revolving arms like windmill sails had already appeared in the locality; but it was looked upon by the men as . . . a farmers' toy; the scythe still did most of the work and they did not dream it would ever be superseded. So while the red sails revolved in one field and the youth on the driver's seat of the machine called cheerily to his horses and women followed behind to bind the corn into sheaves, in the next field a band of men would be whetting their scythes and mowing by hand as their fathers had done before them.

With no idea that they were at the end of a long tradition, they still kept up the old country custom of choosing as their leader the tallest and most highly skilled man amongst them, who was then called 'King of the Mowers' . . .

With a wreath of poppies and green bindweed trails around his wide, rush-plaited hat, he led the band down the swathes as they mowed and decreed when and for how long they should halt for a 'breather' and what drinks should be had from the yellow stone jar they kept under the hedge in a shady corner of the field. They did not rest often or long; for every morning they set themselves to accomplish an amount of work in the day that they knew would tax all their powers till long after sunset. 'Set yourself more than you can do and you'll do it' was one of their maxims, and some of their feats in the harvest field astonished themselves as well as the onlooker . . .

After the mowing and reaping and binding came the carrying, the busiest time of all. Every man and boy put his best foot forward then, for, when the corn was cut and dried it was imperative to get it stacked and thatched before the weather broke. All day and far into the twilight the yellow-and-blue painted farm wagons passed and repassed along

the roads between the field and the stack-yard. Big cart-horses returning with an empty wagon were made to gallop like two-year-olds. Straws hung on the roadside hedges and many a gate-post was knocked down through hasty driving. In the fields men pitchforked the sheaves to the one who was building the load on the wagon, and the air resounded with *Hold tights* and *Wert ups* and *Who-o-oas*. The *Hold tight!* was no empty cry; sometimes, in the past, the man on top of the load had not held tight or not tight enough. There were tales of fathers and grandfathers whose necks or backs had been broken by a fall from a load, and of other fatal accidents afield, bad cuts from scythes, pitchforks passing through feet, to be followed by lockjaw, and of sunstroke; but, happily, nothing of this kind happened on that particular farm in the eighties.

At last, in the cool dusk of an August evening, the last load was brought in, with a nest of merry boys' faces among the sheaves on top, and the men walking alongside with pitchforks on shoulders. As they passed along the roads they shouted:

Harvest home! Harvest home!
Merry, merry, merry harvest home!

And women came to their cottage gates and waved, and the few passers-by looked up and smiled their congratulations . . .
As they approached the farm-house their song changed to:

Harvest home! Harvest home!
Merry, merry, merry harvest home!
Our bottles are empty, our barrels won't run,
And we think it's a very dry harvest home.

And the farmer came out, followed by his daughters and maids with jugs and bottles and mugs, and drinks were handed round amidst general congratulations. Then the farmer invited the men to his harvest home dinner to be held in a few days' time, and the adult workers dispersed to add up their harvest money and to rest their weary bones. The boys and youths, who could never have too much

of a good thing, spent the rest of the evening circling the hamlet and shouting 'Merry, merry, merry harvest home!' until the stars came out and at last silence fell upon the fat rickyard and the stripped fields.

On the morning of the harvest home dinner everybody prepared themselves for a tremendous feast, some to the extent of going without breakfast, that the appetite might not be impaired. And what a feast it was! Such a bustling in the farmhouse kitchen for days beforehand; such boiling of hams and roasting of sirloins; such a stacking of plum puddings, made by the Christmas recipe: such a tapping of eighteen-gallon casks and baking of plum loaves would astonish those accustomed to the appetites of to-day. By noon the whole parish had assembled, the workers and their wives and children to feast and the sprinkling of the better-to-do to help with the serving . . .

Long tables were laid out of doors in the shade of a barn, and soon after twelve o'clock the cottagers sat down to the good cheer, with the farmer carving at the principal table, his wife with her tea urn at another, the daughters of the house with vegetable dishes and beer jugs, and the grandchildren, in their stiff, white, embroidered frocks, dashing hither and thither to see that everybody had what they required. As a background there was the rick-yard with its new yellow stacks and, over all, the mellow sunshine of late summer.

Passers-by on the road stopped their gigs and high dog-carts to wave greetings and shout congratulations on the weather. If a tramp looked wistfully in, he was beckoned to a seat on the straw beneath a rick and a full plate was placed on his knees. It was a picture of plenty and goodwill.'

See also January 25th, September page 11 and song on page 15.

August

19 August

Most of us are quite used to looking at photographs, and even taking them. It is difficult to imagine how magical the first photograph must have seemed when it was taken more than 160 years ago. Until then, the only way anyone could record what an object looked like was by drawing or painting it. With a photograph, it was for the first time possible to capture an image of things exactly as they were – not just as an artist saw them.

The first camera was called a daguerreotype, after the Frenchman who invented it, Jacques Daguerre. On this day in 1839, nearly 150 years ago, he first told people all about his new invention. So today is really the birthday of photography.

People were amazed by his new machine. The whole idea of being able to record the real world, exactly as they saw it, fascinated them. Here's how one Frenchman described it at the time:

'. . . shops were crowded with amateurs panting for daguerreotype apparatus, and everywhere cameras were trained on buildings. Everyone wanted to record the view from his window, and he was lucky who at first trial got a silhouette of roof tops against the sky. He went into ecstasies over chimneys, counted over and over the roof tiles and chimney bricks, was astonished to see the very mortar between the bricks – in a word, the technique was so new that even the poorest proof gave him indescribable joy.'

These early photographs were not made on paper, but on large metal plates. The world's first successful photograph had been made fifteen years earlier, and needed eight hours of light on a summer's day to be taken. It was made by another Frenchman, Joseph Niépce, and he called it a 'sun drawing'. It showed the view from his workroom

window – a pigeon house, pear tree and patch of sky, the roof of a barn and part of a house.

But there was one problem with these early photographs – no copies could be made of them. There was only ever one picture of each object.

It was an Englishman, William Henry Fox Talbot, who succeeded in working out how to take photographs from which copies could be made. It all started while he was on holiday in Italy. He thought how pleasant it would be to record the beauty of the landscape exactly as it was, on paper,

and have it stay there so he could look at it when he was home again. The idea of taking holiday snapshots was quite revolutionary!

Before long he had made a photograph on paper, and had found a way of fixing it there; that is, it would stay on the paper and not blacken the moment any light shone on it.

His first pictures were made by laying plants, lace and feathers on photographic paper and shining light on them. Where the light shone directly onto the paper, the paper turned black. But where it was covered by the plant (for example), it stayed white. Beautiful black and white patterns were made.

Before long, Talbot was using a camera to capture the beauty of the gardens at his home. This was the beginning of photography as we know it nowadays.

Early cameras were very large, bulky objects, made of wood. They always had to be supported on a table or on legs. For this reason, they were difficult to transport, and most people never tried to use one. There was even one camera so big it had to be mounted on wheels and drawn by a horse!

Yet in another 40 years there had been so many improvements that people were already using cameras for holiday snapshots and family pictures. There was a popular craze for what were called 'detective cameras'. These were very small and could be hidden in luggage, paper parcels, hats, ties, underneath waistcoats, handles of walking sticks, disguised to look like binoculars, revolvers, books and watches.

Nowadays, of course, photographs can be taken under almost any conditions, including underwater. And they only take an instant to make. Rather different from the eight hours it took Niépce to make his first 'sun drawing' over 160 years ago!

In some years the following festivals may occur in September:

Janmashtami (Hindu festival). ▶F&F.

Rosh Hashanah (Jewish festival). ▶F&F.

Yom Kippur (Jewish festival). ▶F&F.

The story of Persephone

Now as summer turns to autumn, we think about the changing seasons – the harvest of crops and fruit, the fall of leaves, how plants and seeds will sleep in the ground through winter months.

People have always told stories about why the seasons change – why warmth gives way to cold and growth to barrenness. These stories often recount a battle between good and evil. In spring good wins, and reigns throughout the summer months. Spring festivals often celebrate this victory. Then evil grows more powerful, and winter comes. In time, evil is overpowered by good again, and spring returns.

There is an ancient Greek story which tells how there were no seasons, once. All the months were times of growth; seeds pushed their shoots above the earth, buds opened, leaves unfurled. Each growing thing followed its own rhythm from seed to shoot, from bud to flower and fruit, then back to seed again. There was no pattern. All the year the earth was bright with colour.

Demeter, goddess of the earth, creator and preserver of the cornfield, tended each shoot and bud with loving care. The whole world glowed with her touch, nursing every growing thing to ripeness. Her daughter, Persephone, danced through the dens of her mother's earth, loved sun and light, touched flowers, breathed perfumes, marvelled at the beauty of everything that grew . . .

Below this earth, there was the underworld, the unlit kingdom of the dead. In the darkness Hades ruled, brother of Zeus the lord of all the gods. Among the spirits, pale shadows fluttering through the deep caverns and dark tunnels of the underworld, the king of death was lonely. The great treasures of the rocks, rubies, diamonds, emeralds, were riches beyond his dreams. They only chilled him. He missed the world above, and he grew bitter in his misery.

Harnessing his black horses to his chariot, he rose to the world above and galloped across it, feeling the sunlight, breathing its air. And people shuddered as the speeding shadow of death passed across the sun.

In the brightness of a poppy field, Hades saw Persephone. The happiness of her young life pierced his soul with longing – could she bring light and hope into the darkness in the caverns of the dead? Swiftly he seized her, and sped from the world into the deathly kingdom far below.

Above, in the living world, only the echo of Persephone's despairing cry hung in the air. The poppies withered, trees shrivelled, for death had breathed on them.

Persephone despaired. She trembled in the icy darkness of the underworld. She begged for freedom. She recoiled in horror from the shadowy ghosts who fluttered in the halls of Hades kingdom.

On earth, Demeter heard her daughter's cry. She fled to where the girl had been, but found no trace of her, only the barren earth, the dying flowers.

Day and night she searched across the earth, crying her daughter's name. She forgot her plants, her flowers, her fruits. Seeds rotted in the ground. Leaves withered, fell. At last she knew the signs of death seen in the field were true. Her daughter had been taken to the place of souls whose lives were gone.

She grew angry now. She forbade the trees to fruit, the herbs and corn to grow. 'Until Persephone returns,' she said, 'the earth will sleep. Nothing will grow.'

Zeus, lord of gods, looked down and saw her anger and despair. He also saw the failing harvests on the land, the starving people, the spirit of famine stalk the earth.

'No living person who has eaten food of the dead may leave their kingdom,' he said. 'This is the law of the gods. If Persephone has eaten nothing in my brother's land, she may return to you.'

But time had passed. Persephone had changed. She still saw her husband's coldness, but she also saw his loneliness, his longing for a living creature who would share his exile in the world below. She ceased to fear him. She tasted food he offered. She swallowed four pomegranate seeds. Demeter learned this, and lost all hope. Now Zeus knew that nothing would receive her love on earth. For ever more it would lie chill and empty, without living thing of any kind. People everywhere would starve and die.

So he decreed to Demeter, 'For every seed Persephone has eaten in the underworld she must stay one month there, with her husband. But this gift I give you: the other months of the year, she may enter the world again and be with you.'

Persephone had eaten four pomegranate seeds. From that time onwards, she lives four months of every year as Hades' Queen. Demeter mourns, and nothing can grow. The earth lies bare and still. But then Persephone climbs to the world again. Demeter's sadness ends. Joy overwhelms her and the world glows with her happiness. She nurses every living thing to ripeness through the summer months. Until the harvest comes. Then Persephone

September

returns again to Hades. Demeter's happiness dies. She mourns her daughter's loss. And all the earth mourns with her.

See also August page 8 and song on page 15.
► MCF

2-6 September

'In 1666, London burned like rotten sticks.' You may know this rhyme. It is about the great fire which raged for four days and nights through the narrow streets and wooden houses of London. By the time it died down, the homes of 100,000 Londoners had burned to the ground.

It started soon after midnight on September 2nd 1666, beginning in a baker's house in Pudding Lane, near the River Thames, just north of London Bridge. In no time, the flames flared westwards, blown by a dry east wind through the wooden warehouses along the river banks; then northwards, engulfing everything in its path and reducing the city to smouldering ash. Londoners fled from the city, dragging carts piled high with any belongings they could seize in their panic to escape the flames.

Here is what an important naval officer, Samuel Pepys, wrote in his diary at the time:

'So near the fire as we could for smoke; and all over the Thames, with one's face in the wind you were almost burned with a shower of firedrops – this is very true – so as houses were burned by these drops and flakes of fire, three or four, nay five or six houses, one from another. When we could endure no more upon the water, we to a little alehouse on the Bankside over against the Three Cranes, and there stayed till it was dark almost and saw the fire grow; and as it grow darker, appeared more and more, and in corners and upon steeples and between churches and houses, as far as we could see up the hill of the City, in a most horrid malicious bloody flame, not like the fine flame of an ordinary fire . . .

We stayed till, it being darkish, we saw the fire as only one entire arch of fire from this to the other side the bridge, and in a bow up the hill, for an arch of above a mile long. It made me weep to see it. The churches, houses, and all on fire and flaming at once, and a horrid noise the flames made, and the cracking of houses at their ruin. So home with a sad heart . . .'

Another eyewitness, Sir John Evelyn, described how 'The burning still rages, and it was now gotten as far as the Inner Temple; all Fleet Streete, the Old Bailey, Ludgate Hill, Warwick Lane, Newgate, Paules Chaine, Watling Streete, now flaming, and most of it reduc'd to ashes; the stones of Paules flew like granados, the mealting lead running downe the streetes in a streame, and the very pavements glowing with fiery rednesse, so as no horse nor man was able to tread on them . . .'

In all, 13,200 houses and 89 churches were burned, and a great deal besides.

But when the fire destroyed it, London was a filthy, disease-ridden city. The year before, 100,000 people had died there from the bubonic plague, a disease carried by rats' fleas from the ships, docks and river mouths. At the height of the plague, as many as 6000 people were dying each week. The great fire wiped out the last traces of this killer disease.

And out of the ruins a very different London arose. It was no longer a dirty medieval city, with narrow streets and decaying wooden houses. A cleaner, more airy place emerged, much of it built in brick and stone, with wider streets, drains, and a better water supply.

Six years later, when most of the rebuilding was finished, some thought it was probably one of the healthiest cities in the world.
See also July page 100.

3 September

In 1751 Parliament crossed 11 days off the calendar. *See* March page 70.

After the flood

This is the time of year when some traditions say that life was beginning again after the great flood described at the beginning of the Bible.

The Hareskin Indians of northwestern Canada tell a rather different story about a flood and what happened afterwards.

There was a wise man who watched the heavy snow that fell in September one year, and knew there was going to be a flood. Such snow should not be falling. In his bones he knew the rains would follow, and then melting snow and rain would swell lakes and rivers to bursting point. All the signs of the air told him that this would happen. The birds and the animals around him seemed to know it, too.

He decided to build a raft, just in case.

But all the people laughed at him. 'Why build a raft?' they said. 'We'll climb the trees!'

The wise man took four logs, made ropes of twisted roots, and built his raft. The snows melted. The rains came down. The rivers swelled and burst their banks. The lakes and seas overflowed. All the land was swallowed and all the people who had only climbed the trees were drowned.

But on the raft, the wise man and his family were safe. So were all the animals he had taken with him. Two of every kind he'd chosen, for he knew the earth would need them when the floods went down.

Days, weeks, months, they drifted on. Then the musk rat said it was time to see if the water was going down. Downward he plunged from the raft. He could not reach the bottom, and rose to the surface, gasping for air.

He caught his breath, then plunged again. This time the scent of the earth reached him, but he could not dive deep enough to touch it.

Next it was the beaver's turn. He was gone for a very long time. Then the other watching animals saw him bob to the surface of the water and float there motionless, exhausted by the dive. But in his paw he clenched some earth.

The wise man took the earth, and sprinkled it across the surface of the water. He blew on it, and said, 'Let there be earth again.'

The sprinkled earth began to grow. He lifted a tiny bird from beside him on the raft, and placed it on the earth. The patch of soil grew more. The wise man blew and blew, and each time the earth grew larger, rounder, across the flood waters.

He said to the fox, 'You run around the earth and see how large it is.' The fox did so. In no more than a single day he'd sped to every corner of the earth. 'Run around again,' the wise man said. Round and round the fox ran; on every circle the earth swelled more, until he had run a full six times. On the seventh, the earth was as big as it had been before the flood.

Then the wise man said, 'Now is the time for all to leave the raft.'

But how to make the floods go down? Now it was the water-bird, the bittern, who offered help. 'Let me swallow the water,' he said, and did so. He fell to the ground, his belly swollen to an enormous size.

Now there was no water anywhere. None for the people or the animals to drink. None for the plants and trees.

The wise man said to the plover, 'Can you help now?' The plover said it could. And with his beak he poked the bittern's belly, hard.

There was a mighty gurgling. Out from the fat bird's belly all the water gushed, and flowed into the rivers and lakes.

Now the earth was in its place, and water was in its place. Life could start again, just as it was before the flood. And so it did.

See also July 27th, April page 80, Class Assembly page 123.

> **Note to readers**
> To refer you to relevant material, including songs, in other Ward Lock Educational books we have used this symbol ▶
> *See* page 4

7 September

On September 7th, 1854, more than 130 years ago, some men decided to take the handle off a water pump in a small side-street in London. By this action, hundreds of people were saved from a disease which, in one year alone, had killed nearly half a million people.

The disease was cholera. In the latest outbreak in Soho, London, nearly 200 people had died only six hours after falling ill. Yet no one knew what caused the illness. Victims were struck down with lightning speed, and within days, sometimes hours, they were dead. The illness was common in the poor areas of the cities, in the stinking, undrained streets, clogged, rotting and oozing with rubbish and lavatory waste.

Some people thought it was spread by touch. Others believed it travelled through the air. Once an epidemic began, nothing seemed to stop it, and no one could prevent the deaths.

But there was help at hand, for there was a quiet, hard-working doctor in Soho who had been studying cholera for many years. His name was Dr John Snow.

Having tended many victims of the disease, he was certain that people caught it from drinking dirty water. Clean water was very hard to find in those days. The houses had no taps, and people had to fetch water from a few street pumps, often some distance away. It was dirty when they fetched it, and even dirtier by the time it had been standing in buckets in their homes, waiting to be used.

When the outbreak struck Soho, Dr Snow began some careful and thorough detective work. He pieced together a map of where and how each cholera patient got their water. And he found that each victim fetched it from the same place – the water pump in Broad Street, Soho.

Then, curiously, a woman and her niece died in

Hampstead, a few miles away. Yet no one else fell ill outside Soho. When Dr Snow investigated further, he discovered that the woman had been particularly fond of the water from the Broad Street pump. She had some brought to her in Hampstead. Within two days of drinking it, she was dead. So was her niece. He needed no other proof.

Dr Snow's answer was simple. Remove the pump handle. People could not then drink the water. The epidemic stopped. There could be no doubt, the disease was passed on through infected water. To drink from the Broad Street pump was the same as drinking a deadly poison.

There is no cholera in Britain today. It took time for Dr Snow's discovery to be accepted, but in the end towns were cleaned up and supplied with pure water and proper drains, so preventing this danger to our health. We have men like Dr Snow to thank for this, and for the saving of millions of lives as a result.

7 September

In 1876 Alexander Graham Bell's telephone was first demonstrated in Britain, in Glasgow.

See October 26th.

National Day in Brazil. ▶ MCF.

The yellow death

Prince Elphin was a most unlucky prince. His powerful father, Gwyddno Garanhir ruled mid-Wales thirteen centuries ago. Yet all the gifts he gave his son went wrong. Even when he told him he could keep all the salmon caught that year, the gift was nothing, for although multitudes were usually netted, that year, not a single fish was caught.

There was, however, a large leather bag found in the river. The river keeper carried it to Elphin. To their astonishment there was a tiny boy inside.

'Tal-iesin!' the keeper said, amazed; that is, 'how his face glows!' for the child's forehead had a strange radiance to it.

So Taliesin became the infant's name. Elphin lifted the child onto his horse and turned for home. Then, in amazement he heard the tiny boy begin to speak in glorious poetry, and tell him wonderful things. He, Taliesin, had been sent to guide the prince. He could help him withstand all enemies and prosper in all he did. He could foretell the future and he knew the fate of kings and men.

His prophecy came true. From that time onwards, Prince Elphin's fortunes changed. He was no longer the unluckiest prince in all Wales' history, but had success in all he did. Taliesin became the most famous bard in Britain.

One of Taliesin's prophecies was how the wicked king Maelgwn Gwynned, chief ruler of all Wales, would meet his end. He was so evil that people cursed him with every breath, yet no one dared to challenge him. The numbers of his victims grew and grew until there was not a man or woman who had not felt his power.

Only Taliesin foretold his doom. 'A monstrous yellow beast will rise from the sea marsh of the maidens,' he said 'Its teeth and eyes and hair will be all yellow, and it will take revenge for all the evil deeds of Maelgwn Gwynned.'

In the year CE 547, a deadly plague known as the yellow death crept across Britain, leaving a trail of dead and dying in its wake. It neared the land of Maelgwn Gwynned. The king's terror grew until he was almost mad with it. He fled into his palace, taking a few favourite courtiers with him, and held the palace like a fort. No one went in or out.

Until one day, he heard his name called loudly from beyond the palace walls. He put his eye to the great keyhole in the outer gate, and looked through it. There came a shriek of pain and fright, and Maelgwn Gwynned fell writhing to the ground. 'The yellow beast,' he whispered hoarsely. And then, in terrible agony, he died.

And so Taliesin's prophecy came true.

12 September

The birthday in 1913, of Jesse Owens, who made sporting history in 1935 and 1936. *See* May 25th.

Note to readers

To refer you to relevant material, including songs, in other Ward Lock Educational books we have used this symbol ▶
See page 4

Harvest song

Words and music by
Jan Holdstock

1 In Great Great Grandfather's day
   He planted out his garden in April and
      May
   With cabbage in the cabbage patch, and
      peaches on the wall;
   In September and October he'd enjoy
      them all.
   *So give thanks to the earth, the rain and
      the sun*
   That grow the food for every one.

2 It's all quite different today!
   Now we can fill our larders the
      supermarket way.
   Our cabbage comes in freezer packs
   And peaches come in tins –
   But we'll still be very glad when Harvest
      Time begins.
   So give thanks to the earth, etc

▶ ECUS No 37
▶ MCF page 82

15

Autumn, autumn, what do you bring?

Words and music by
Eileen Diamond

1 Autumn, autumn, what do you bring?
Days that are mellow and
Leaves turning yellow.
Oh, autumn, autumn, when will you
come?
After the summer,
When summer has gone.

2 Autumn, autumn, what will you show?
Fields full of corn
And a mist in the morning.
Oh, autumn, autumn, when will you
come? etc.

3 Autumn, autumn, how will we know?
Days will be shorter
The year's passed three quarter.
Oh, autumn, autumn, when will you
come? etc.

▶ECUS No 4

16

15 September

There were once quite a few people who thought it was outlandish nonsense to think that there could ever be any kind of transport other than the horse.

One doctor said the human body would collapse if it was forced to move through air at any speed above that of a galloping horse. Others said the brain would be injured. Another, that as soon as a train entered a tunnel, all the passengers would suffocate and die.

When the railways first began to appear in Britain, many farmers were also against them, for they said the cattle would be frightened and stop producing milk.

But there were also many people who greeted the arrival of the railways with great excitement. On this day in 1830 the first public passenger railway – a 46 kilometre line from Manchester to Liverpool – was opened. 50,000 spectators gathered to watch. One of the first passengers that day was Fanny Kemble, a famous actress. She wrote:

'The most intense curiosity and excitement prevailed . . . Enormous masses of densely packed people lined the road, shouting and waving hats and handkerchiefs, as we flew by them. What with the sight of those cheering multitudes and the tremendous (speed) with which we were borne past them, my spirits rose to champaigne height . . .'

Earlier, after one of the trial runs, she had also described the sense of speed:

'The engine set off at its utmost speed, 35 miles (56km) per hour, swifter than a bird flies. You cannot conceive what that sensation of cutting the air was . . . this sensation of flying was quite delightful and strange beyond description . . .'

These speeds, which seem nothing to us nowadays, were very frightening to many. One Member of Parliament, who had travelled for eight kilometres at a speed of 32 kilometres an hour, said,

'It is impossible to divest yourself of the notion of instant death to all upon the least accident happening. It gave me a headache which has not left me yet. Altogether I am extremely glad to have seen this miracle, and to have travelled in it. But, having done so, I am quite satisfied with my first achievement being my last.'

The newspapers did nothing to calm people's fears. One wrote:

'Does anybody mean to say that decent people would consent to be hurried along through the air upon a railroad, from which, had a lazy schoolboy left a marble, or a wicked one a stone, they would be pitched off their perilous track into the valley beneath; or is it to be imagined that women would endure the fatigue, and misery, and danger, not only to themselves, but their children and families, of being dragged through the air at the rate of twenty miles an hour, all their lives being at the mercy of a tin pipe, or a copper boiler, or the accidental dropping of a pebble on the line of way.'

To some, the shock of the railways was that 'grave plodding citizens will be flying about like comets.'

Despite all opposition and fears, the new railways spread rapidly in the twenty years that followed the opening of the Manchester to Liverpool railway. They cut the time taken to travel distances to less than a third of that taken by stage coaches. In 1845 there were 3680 kilometres of railway open. Seven years later it was three times as much, and the lives of many of the people were transformed. Now they could make journeys they would never have undertaken before.

16 September

Independence Day in Mexico, Papua and New Guinea. ▶MCF.

17 September

Charles Darwin reached the Galapagos Islands. *See* January page 51.

Yam Festival in Ghana. ▶MCF.

September

28 September

There was once a man who was fascinated by the tiny living creatures he could see using a microscope. He kept asking himself, where do they come from, what makes them grow?

He made meat soup, and let it go bad. There were millions of them in the rotten soup! He took some from sour milk and put them in fresh milk. They grew and grew, and produced millions of other creatures just like themselves. He struggled up the slippery precipices of a great mountain glacier, just to find out if the mountain air also had these things in it, and how many.

And he discovered something so important that all our lives would be totally different without it. Many of us would probably not even be alive.

You probably know who the man is, without realising it, for you have him to thank each time you drink a glass of pure milk. He developed the method we use for killing bacteria in milk, and it was called 'pasteurising' after him. For the man was Louis Pasteur, a French scientist who made all these discoveries more than 120 years ago.

Pasteur found that many of the creatures swarming in his liquids were the things we call bacteria. He worked out that these bacteria make us ill when they invade our bodies in large numbers. At that time, this was a totally new and startling idea. Doctors then were not able to cure or prevent most illnesses. Sometimes they could lessen the suffering of sick people, just a little. But, usually, they had to let diseases run their course, until the patient either became well again, or died.

On the other hand, once doctors knew from Pasteur that it was bacteria causing many of the illnesses, their work was transformed. For the first time they could really start to fight disease. They could track down the harmful bacteria and destroy them.

Pasteur made many brilliant discoveries while trying to find out what was killing all the silkworms in France's rich silk industry. He learned other important things while investigating killer diseases among poultry and cattle.

He became particularly famous when his understanding of microscopic creatures led him to develop a cure for the dreaded rabies. Until Pasteur's cure, people always died from this terrible disease caught from the bite of a mad dog.

Pasteur died on this day in 1895. Yet his achievements live on. They are among the greatest discoveries ever made, and they are at the heart of the work of doctors and nurses, healing and caring for the sick all over the world.

'They took our land'

'The Great Spirit raised both the white man and the Indian, I think he raised the Indian first. He raised me in this land and it belongs to me. The white man was raised over the great waters, and his land is over there. Since they crossed the sea, I have given them room. There are now white people all about me. I have but a small spot of land left. The Great Spirit told me to keep it' . . . 'They made us many promises, more than I can remember, but they never kept but one; they promised to take our land, and they took it.'

These are the words of Red Cloud, chief of the Sioux Indian nation during the 1860s, last century. He is telling, with bitterness, of the European settlers in America, moving westwards in pursuit of land and Californian gold, invading and stealing all the land on which the Indians had lived for thousands of years.

The settlers pushed right into the centre of what had been agreed by treaty was Indian territory. For the Indian peoples, life was bound to the earth and all its riches – land and animals, birds and plants. They had seen the forests of the east of America felled beneath the axes of millions of settlers. They had seen the steady march of these newcomers, changing, destroying everything in their path.

Now they were expected to accept the seizure of their land, and brutality and cruelty from both settler and the American army which is too nightmarish to recount.

Another Sioux chief, Spotted Tail, said this; (talking of America's President as the Great Father), 'This war did not spring up here in our land, this war was brought upon us by the children of the Great Father who came to take our land from us without price, and who, in our land, do a great many evil things. The Great Father and his children are to blame for this trouble . . . It has been our wish to live here in our country peaceably, and do such things as may be for the good of our people, but the Great Father has filled it with soldiers who think only of our death.'

They tried to withstand the tide of the settlers' march into their lands. The Navahos and Apaches, the Cheyenne and the Sioux fought back as long as they had chiefs to lead them into battle – famous men like Cochise, Geronimo, Crazy Horse, Sitting Bull and Red Cloud.

They fought with great courage and great skill, but it was against overwhelming odds. In the end, torn from their traditional way of life, thousands dead from famine and disease, they ended their days herded into reservations in the land which had been their own. The conquest of the settlers was complete.

Much of the history of these years is found in the records of treaty councils, where Indian leaders met to negotiate the holding of land with government officials. There the Indians spoke about their history, their way of life, and of their deep feeling

Our first woman doctor

When a young woman named Elizabeth Garrett announced to her mother that she was going to become a doctor, her mother hid herself in her bedroom and wept for shame.

It was bad enough that her daughter stooped so low as to want to earn a living, but to want to become a *doctor* was even worse!

About 100 years ago, this was the kind of reaction many people had, to the idea of women taking their part as equals alongside men. People believed they would be too stupid to learn, or too weak to do the work. Or they considered that this kind of work was far too undignified for a well brought-up young lady.

Women were not allowed to study at any medical school. Nor were they allowed to take the examinations to qualify as a doctor.

So Elizabeth Garrett prepared for what she knew would be a long struggle to achieve her aim. Her first success came in 1860 – she was allowed to start studying at the Middlesex Hospital in London. Really, the doctor there was certain that when she went into a surgical ward, experienced the sights, sounds and smells, she would be so appalled that she would give up the whole idea of becoming a doctor.

Elizabeth did not. After a while she was working so well, that she won the chance to attend lectures. One day, the male students were asked a question by the lecturer. Not one of them was able to answer him. Elizabeth could. The other students were so angry at this, that they insisted she should not be allowed to come to lectures again. But Elizabeth refused to despair. She simply continued studying privately, despite all the insults and opposition she continually faced. In the end, she succeeded, and she became the first woman doctor in Britain.

In 1872, she opened the New Hospital for Women, in London, later renamed the Elizabeth Garrett Anderson hospital, (Anderson was her married name). The following year, she became a member of the British Medical Association, the organisation which controlled the work of doctors throughout Britain.

However, when Elizabeth attended her first meeting, there was an uproar. Women in the British Medical Association! Elizabeth refused to leave. So the Association simply made a new rule – that no other woman could become a member. For 19 years Elizabeth was the only woman there.

Yet the insults and rough treatment which she had to put up with were nothing compared with the problems that the first woman doctor in Scotland, Sophia Jex-Blake, had. She and a group of women embarked on a long struggle to qualify as doctors. Even when they finally succeeded, students let sheep loose in the hall during the group's qualifying ceremony.

Both Sophia and Elizabeth had been inspired by the efforts of another woman, Elizabeth Blackwell, who was the first woman doctor ever to practise. She became a doctor in America, but only after one school after another had turned her down. Even when she had all the necessary training, no hospital would allow her to work. Landladies in New York refused to rent her a room, and many of New York's women turned their backs on her when she walked by, or insulted her to her face when they were forced to meet.

Because of the efforts of these women, Parliament was forced to make a new law, allowing women to take the qualifying examinations to become doctors. Like all the many people who have fought in the past for equal rights for women, we have a lot to thank these pioneering doctors for.

for the land which the settlers wanted to take from them.

The history of these years, of what was done to the Indian peoples of America is a tragic one. You will not find it portrayed in many films or stories. But it is true, nevertheless.

September

30 September

In 1929 the BBC made its first television broadcast to the public. *See* January 27th.

Moon festival

Chinese people celebrate an autumn harvest festival called the Festival of the Moon Goddess, and sometimes the Mooncake Festival, because special cakes are made to be eaten and offered to the moon. Here is one of the stories remembered at this time.

Ch'ang-o was wife of I, the miraculous archer, he who had shot his magic arrows and brought down the nine suns which rose together, shrivelling up the world beneath their burning glare.

Many other deeds of bravery had been performed by him, and so the gods gave him the drug of immortality – a medicine so powerful that if he swallowed a single tablet he would never die, but live for ever, and would be able to fly to the end of the world and back.

He hid this precious gift beneath the rafters of his house. One day, his wife Ch'ang-o was alone in the house. She noticed a strange perfume in the air, new, delightful, and enticing. At once she forgot all else, and began to search all through her home to find the source of this unusual fragrance. She reached the room where I had hidden the tablet of immortality. She saw a white light shining from the rafter above her head.

At once, she fetched a ladder, and climbed up to have a look. There was the white tablet, in its hiding place. A desperate urge to swallow it overwhelmed her. Barely knowing what she did, she put it in her mouth, and it was at once as though she was going to float into the air, so light and airy she felt.

Just then, she heard the footsteps of her husband in the house. He entered the room, and saw that she had taken the tablet of immortality.

Ch'ang-o fled, leaping through the window to escape his anger. But instead of falling to her death below, she found herself flying up into the sky, upwards and upwards, beyond the clouds, until she reached the silvery circle of the moon. There she has lived, ever since, immortal, a goddess, her beauty shining down upon the world for ever more.

And I, his anger calmed, travels to visit her on the fifteenth day of every moon. Which is why the moon shines particularly brightly on this day.

▶ MCF and F&F.

In some years the following festivals may fall in October:

Birthday of Muhammad. *See* November page 38.

White Sunday in Samoa. ▶MCF.

First Monday in October

Today is United Nations Universal Childrens' Day, dedicated to children all over the world. A few years ago journalists talked to children from five continents about their lives, their hopes, and their wishes for the future. Here are some of the things said by children – from very different countries, in very different parts of the world:

A great many of the world's children live in country areas, working on the land:

'I work on this farm. I like doing most of the jobs, well, all of the jobs that I'm asked to do. I prefer to be at school to working here, but the family needs the money so I have to work. I work from 7 o'clock in the morning here until 4 o'clock in the afternoon . . .

When I left the school it was obvious I had to leave because I couldn't afford the money for the books. There were lots of other children in much the same position, they had to leave the school too. But now I'm working, that means that my brothers and sisters can stay at school because I can earn money to help them. Now my other brothers and sisters will be able to stay at school much longer than I did, and I am pleased about that.

As for me, it just wasn't possible for me to stay. The only money that comes into our house is what I earn here at the vegetable garden and what my mother earns milking the cows . . .'

'We have 20 acres of dry land. With uncles and aunts there are 20 of us altogether in the family. I have to work on someone else's farm for wages . . . I've never been to school. I don't understand it. My mother is not strong and she can't manage the work so I have to stay.

'I have a little land for myself and I plant bananas, yams, cassava, cocoa and coffee. My grandfather tells me what to do. He is a good farmer. I watched him and he showed me how. I have been farming since I was seven years old.'

Throughout the world there are millions of children who live on the streets, scratching a living in any way they can:

'I am nine years old. A lot of people call me a small boy, but I live alone. My work is that I sell chewing gum around the Orion Circle at cinema time . . . I don't go to school. I don't go because I don't have money. I have no sleeping house. I sleep at the lorry petrol station.'

'Sometimes we beg for money. Other times we begged for scraps of food from the cafes . . . My mother didn't mind when I left. There isn't room for me at home and she can't feed me. Besides, she knows I can look after myself .. I did go to school for a while . . . But my mother didn't get enough money to buy food every day so I left to do washing dishes in the cafe to help get money.'

'Sometimes no-one wants shoes shining and I can't buy anything to eat. But you can always find scraps in garbage cans and drink tea that people leave over at cafés on the road . . .'

'I sleep anywhere sheltered, under a bridge or a bus stand . . . When I'm older I'm going into business. I'll sell fruit and vegetables . . .

It's a good business. I'll be a good business man because I have learned to look after myself.'

'I am looking through all this rubbish every day. It is my work. I am nine years old. I look for glass, paper, old iron things, plastic sandals. My brothers showed me how. They have done it for a long time . . . I don't like this work. You work in the sun all day. You get dirty. You get sick easy. There is no other work to get money for family . . .

We sleep outside. If it rains we sleep inside hut. Roof leaks onto sacking. We put tins to collect water.

I would like to go to school. I like to see small girls going to school with books and slate . . .

We get water from tap. There is queue every morning. We have to wait one hour. We get one pitcher of water. When I finish working at night there is only water left for hands and face. So we stay dirty from rubbish at night.

Life will be better when I am older. I will work on building site and earn money. I would like to have a house and two sets of clothes. I would like to have a proper house so we can always stay there. I do not like to keep moving.'

How do children around the world foresee the future? The year 2000, for example – what do they think will be happening then? And what would they *like* to happen?

'In the year 2000 I would be 38. There is every possibility that I may not still be alive. But if I am, I will be an architect. I want to build buildings which will not only beautify the world but bring happiness. People who live in my buildings cannot help but smile and be happy.'

'In 2000 AD I will be a farmer. I will have a dip and fences for my cattle. I will have crop rotation and fertilisers. I hope to do a lot for the country so everyone will have a lot of food.'

'I don't want to be rich. People just envy you.

October

Words and music by
Barrie Carson Turner

'Why should you have more than you need? Once you've got a home, family, friends and a job you should be satisfied.'

'In the year 2000, an operation for cancer will be childishly simple and certain words like 'war' will have been forgotten.'

'We will stop industry, which keeps going deeper and deeper into nature, and save from extinction all rare species and help animals to live in the wilderness.'

'The day will begin with breakfast prepared by robots. Dishes will be in pills – a red pill for tea, a brown one for bread, and a white one for milk. Lessons in school will be taught by robots as well. Every school child will have a device like a tape-recorder which will record what the robot-teacher says so you don't have to remember it. Bedtime stories will be about the old times on Earth when people drove cars and motor-bikes and killed each other.'

'There will not be beggars and poor people. Everyone will have jobs and food.'

'In the year 2000 I want there to be peace and I want all parents to be like mine, to understand their children and not beat them.'

'When we are adults the United Nations will be even stronger. Then it will order all countries to get rid of weapons which can extinguish life on earth.'

'I aspire that in the year 2000 there will be one nation, and that is human beings; that there is one race and that is the human race; and there is one religion and that is humanity; and that there is one country and that is the earth; and lastly that the entire mankind may lead a harmonious life of peaceful existence and tolerance.'

New Internationalist

See song on page 88.

Hibernating time

Winds are strong, the skies are grey,
Colder weather day by day,
Now lots of animals hide away—
It's hibernating time again.
Nights grow very, very cold,
Days are short—the year is old,
Time when the animals sleep and wait
For springtime again.

1. Frogs and toads and newts and snakes
   Vanish when the weather breaks.
   They will find a cosy space
   In a dry and sheltered place.
   Bats enjoy their yearly rest,
   Hanging upside down—you've guessed;
   Hedgehogs through the gardens roam,
   Searching for their winter home.

   Winds are strong etc.

2. Squirrels bury underground
   Lots of woodland food they've found,
   Keep it for a winter day
   When they wake inside their dray.
   We've not mentioned tortoise yet,
   Children keep him as a pet,
   Likes to hibernate as well
   Tightly curled inside his shell.

   Winds are strong, etc.

23

year - ly rest, Hang - ing up - side down — you've guessed,

Hedge - hogs through the gar - dens roam, Search - ing for their

win - ter home. shell.

2 October

Darwin's *HMS Beagle* reached England after five years' voyage. *See* January page 51.

United and strong

There was once a man with several sons, who were continually arguing with each other. Every day brought a new quarrel about this or that, and no matter how hard the father tried, he could not get them to live and work together peacefully.

At last he made up his mind to show them how foolish they were being. He told them to fetch some sticks and, taking them, he bound them in a bundle. This he gave to each of the sons in turn, asking him to snap the bundle across his knee. Each son tried, and each son failed.

Then the man untied the bundle and separated the sticks, passing them to his sons one by one.

Now they could break the sticks quite easily.

'You see, my sons,' he said, 'Together you will always be able to withstand any attack. But if you quarrel with each other and pull apart, you will never have any strength and will always be weak in the face of any enemy.'

Strength is found in unity.   *Adapted from Aesop*

7 October

National Day in Germany. ▶MCF.

11 October

It was late evening on board the *Santa Maria*, October 11th 1492. The ship's commander, Christopher Columbus, felt in his bones, saw by all the signs of sea and air, that they were near to land. It would be the first land they had sighted since they left the Canary Islands in the Atlantic Ocean, 35 days before. Since then they had been steering west across waters that were quite unknown to them.

The voyage had been a very difficult one, for among the seamen there had been terrible fears that they would never reach dry land again. They had begun to think they would all die. The ship had been becalmed in the Sargasso Sea, in seaweed so thick it seemed as though it would be caught for ever more. Several times they had seen mountains rising from the sea. But they had turned out to be only clouds, and so their disappointment was bitter and their fears grew and grew. Now many were becoming mutinous and saying that their commander, Columbus, was mad.

But now Columbus was convinced he saw a light ahead of him 'like a wax candle that rose and fell.' Dawn proved him right. It showed a rocky coast, with beautiful wooded hills beyond. Cautiously the ship moved along the shore, looking for somewhere to anchor.

And from the shore, eyes watched them, the eyes of the inhabitants of this island, now seeing their first glimpse of the men from across the oceans who would seize their land, change the whole face of the vast continent they had reached, and redraw the map of the world for ever more.

The following morning, Columbus and his crew went ashore, and in a solemn ceremony they 'took possession of the island' in the name of the Spanish King and Queen, for whom Columbus had made this voyage of exploration.

This day is often described in the history books as 'the discovery of America'. It was, of course, no such thing, for the islands off the coast and the whole continents of North and South America had been discovered thousands of years before, by all the ancestors of the people who were living in that land when Columbus and his sailors first set foot on it.

It *was* a voyage of discovery for the Spaniards, to a land which neither they, nor most other European nations had known was there. Columbus himself was convinced that he had reached the Indies, the islands off the coast of India, which Marco Polo had visited on his voyage from China to India. Columbus believed that the great continent nearby was India, and did not realise it was quite another land, as yet unnamed by Europeans. He called the inhabitants 'Indians', and the name has stuck ever since.

The arrival of Columbus there is often also called the discovery of America by white men, or the discovery of America by Europeans. But in 1961 an ancient settlement was found in Newfoundland,

Columbus after landing

Canada. At first it was thought to be an Indian village, but then, to everyone's surprise, it turned out to be a Viking settlement. There were some very old stories about Vikings reaching America many years ago. Now it seemed as though these stories were true. The legends, the Saga of Erik the Red, tell how the Viking leader, Leif Erikson, landed on the continent around CE 1000 (about 492 years before Columbus). There is another account, written in CE 1070 by someone who spent some time at the court of the Danish King. He tells of common knowledge of 'another island (other than Iceland and Greenland) which many had discovered in that ocean, and which is called 'Vinland' because vines grow . . . and produce excellent wine. This we know not from fables . . . but from reliable information from the Danes.'

There was also a Welsh prince, Madoc, in the twelfth century, who had long wanted to sail westwards from the shores of Wales, until he reached another land beyond the ocean. He set out with a crew of sailors in CE 1170. Nothing was heard of him for several years. Then he returned. Only a few sailors were now on board. The rest, he said, had been left in the new land which they had discovered after many weeks sailing across the sea.

Prince Madoc stayed just long enough to prepare a fleet of ships and find men and women who wanted to sail back with him. They departed, and that was the last ever heard of them.

Six hundred years later, settlers going into North America in the seventeenth and eighteenth centuries, heard of a tribe of Indians called the Mandans. They were supposed to be white-skinned and spoke a language rather like Welsh. Then other records of the tribe were found. Now many people believed that Prince Madoc *did* land in Alabama in 1170 and so reached the continent of North America more than 300 years before Columbus.

October

12 October

On this day in 1982, the wreck of the Tudor ship *Mary Rose* was raised from the seabed where she had been buried for more than 435 years. She sank during a battle against the French fleet on July 19th, 1545, but without being hit by any French guns. Why she sank is still a mystery. Some said that it was because of the weight of her guns, for she was the most heavily-armed warship of that time.

The fleet of French ships was nearing the south coast of England near the Isle of Wight. A much smaller English fleet sailed out to challenge it. But before the *Mary Rose*, the vice-flagship and the pride of the English fleet, could fire a single shot, she sank with 700 men on board.

Some accounts written at the time said that she capsized accidentally because her crew were careless and undisciplined. But the ship's officers were all lost, her captain too, and so was the vice-admiral, Sir George Carew. So there was no one left alive who could say what had really happened.

The younger brother of the vice-admiral, Sir Peter Carew, told how the ship began to tilt badly as soon as the crew began to haul up the sail. Water poured through the gun ports which were all open, ready to fire upon the French. She began to sink, rapidly. Fewer than three dozen men out of the 700 escaped the ship. (If it was true that she had 700 men on board, then she was a lot more heavily loaded than usual. The usual number would have been 415 men.)

Immediately after the battle, people tried to salvage the ship. But in the end they gave up. Years went by, and everyone forgot the *Mary Rose*. Three hundred years later, fishermen found they frequently caught their nets on something at the bottom of the sea. They told some men who were diving in the area. Down the divers went to have a look. They brought up some brass cannon and smaller objects from the wreck. Then, again, the *Mary Rose* was forgotten.

More than 130 years later, efforts to find her began again. This time, the searchers used modern equipment, which could tell by sounds bouncing off objects under water whether there was anything unexpected down there. After two years' work, they found the wreck. The slow, careful work began, uncovering her and bringing objects to the surface to be studied.

One of the problems in raising something from the seabed where it has been preserved in sand for so long, is that the moment it is moved, it starts to break up. One of the very important tasks was to find ways of treating the objects to prevent them from decaying.

At last, in 1982, the final stage of discovery took place. The *Mary Rose* was triumphantly raised to the surface, to end her days in the naval docks at Portsmouth where you can go and visit her.

The making of the world

This is one of the ancient stories from the Scandinavian countries which tells of the creation of the world, and of the first rainbow.

At the dawn of time, there was nothing – no sea, no earth, only an abyss, a yawning emptiness, stretching for ever more. Then, to the north, formed Niflheim, a shadowy region of clouds and mists, and in the centre rose the great fountain from which flowed the waters of twelve icy rivers.

To the south formed Muspelheim, the land of fire. From its burning regions poured a fiery liquid, so that there came a time when the icy waters of Niflheim and the burning streams of Muspelheim mingled, hardened, and, frost covered, began to fill the bottomless gorge between.

All the while the hot winds blew from Muspelheim, and the ice in the abyss began to melt. From it rose the first living being, a giant, Ymir; from him other giants were born and the race of giants began to rule the universe.

Out of the melting ice burst the cow, Audumla, to nurse the giants with her rich milk. She licked the ice; another form began to show beneath its frozen surface. Hair, then a head, a neck, shoulders emerged. Then the whole body of a god, Buri, the first of the race of gods.

Buri had a son, Bor. Bor married a daughter of Ymir, and she gave birth to the three gods Odin, Vili, Ve, gigantic beings who had the strength of giants and the power of gods.

God now fought giant to rule the universe – a bloody bitter struggle: on the one hand Ymir and the giants; on the other the sons of Bor – Odin, Vili, Ve. A thousand centuries the battle raged, never ceasing, until at last Ymir grew old and tired. His strength began to fail him, and it was now that the sons of Bor gave him his death blow.

They raised his vanquished body high and from it formed the earth. They called it Midgard, the middle dwelling, for it was halfway between the land of fire and the land of ice.

His blood became the sea, his bones the mountains and his hair the trees. His skull, raised high on pillars, formed the arching heavens. Then the gods took sparks which flew out of Muspelheim and with them made the sun, the moon, the stars.

Then they built their home high in the heavens and they called it Asgard. Between Asgard, the royal home of gods, and Midgard, the earth, they built a bridge – the many-coloured arch of the first rainbow.

In time, three gods, Odin, Hoenir and Lodur, were travelling across the earth. It was deserted, without living creature on it. They saw two lifeless trunks of trees, dead, twisted logs of driftwood.

From each they carved a living doll, and Odin breathed life into them, Hoenir a thinking mind, and Lodur the colour of a living being. The one, a woman, they named Embla; the other, a man, they named Ask.

And so the race of giants and the race of gods were joined now by the first of the race of people – the founders of the race of human beings.

See also January 28th, May page 85.

15 October

Have you ever heard someone called a 'Mata Hari'? It is a name which usually means that someone is a spy.

It comes from a real person who lived at the beginning of this century. She is very famous, but also really very mysterious. People believed she spied for the Germans during the First World War. She was tried by the French, found guilty, and shot in 1917. But there are some people who think she never was a spy, and was quite wrongly executed.

Her real name was Margaretha Gertruida Zelle, and she was Dutch. She had lived for a while in the East Indies, and there she saw many beautiful, exotic dances, which she later copied when she earned her living in Europe as a dancer on the stage. She chose 'Mata Hari' as her stage name, which means 'The eye of the dawn'.

It wasn't long before rumours began about her being a spy. Many of her friends were French army officers, and some of them were very senior. People said that she gathered important army secrets from them and passed them to the Germans, who paid her well for it.

In the end she was arrested, charged with spying and tried by the French military court – a court martial. She was shot on October 15th, 1917.

But *had* she been spying? We don't really know for sure. She always said that she had never done

so, and had never harmed the allied armies of France and England in any way. According to some, the military court never properly proved the charges against her.

We shall probably never know the truth of the story. But it is sad to think she may have been punished for something she never did.

18 October

St Luke's Day. *See* Class Assembly page 114.

Hearing the truth

In 1854, Britain and France went to war with Russia. The war was fought many miles from Britain's shores, on a penisular in the Black Sea, called the Crimea.

But it could not for long remain a distant war for the people of Britain. For the first time they were able to read eye-witness accounts of the battle front, written by someone there, watching the fighting, living in the camps, observing the hospitals.

They were the writings of a journalist, William Howard Russell of the *The Times* newspaper. From the reports he sent back, people learned not only about the determination and courage of the British soldiers, but also of their misery and pain, their wounds, the pointless loss of lives. Soldiers were dying not only in the heat of battle, but also after, from neglect and filth, dying for want of medicines and medical equipment, dying even for want of clothes.

People would have expected to hear descriptions of neat, clean army camps, with orderly tents, groomed horses, smart uniforms. Instead Russell wrote of:

'a vast black dreary wilderness of mud, dotted with little lochs of foul water and seamed by dirty brownish and tawny-coloured streams running

The Crimean winter

down to and along the ravines. On its surface everywhere are strewn the carcasses of horses and miserable animals torn by dogs and smothered by mud. Vultures swoop over the mounds in flocks . . .'

The more Russell saw, the angrier he became. 'It is with feelings of surprise and anger that the public will learn that no sufficient preparations have been made for the care of the wounded . . . men must die through the medical staff of the British Army having forgotten that old rags are necessary

October

for the dressing of wounds.'

On another occasion he reported:

'It is now pouring rain and the skies are as black as ink – the wind is howling over the staggering tents – the trenches are turned into dykes – in the tents the water is sometimes a foot deep – our men have not either warm or waterproof clothing – they are out for twelve hours at a time in the trenches . . . and not a soul seems to care for their comfort or even for their lives . . . These are the foul truths, but the people of England must hear them.'

The people of England did hear them. They were unable to ignore what Russell told them. They did not demand an end to the war, but they did demand that something be done to lessen the suffering of soldiers there.

Florence Nightingale and her team of nurses were sent out to the Crimea, to improve the care of the wounded in the hospital. *The Times* newspaper organised a fund for donations, so that supplies of

equipment, medicine, and all the other things so badly needed could be sent to them.

Without Russell's reports none of this would have happened. Up till then, people only heard what the army and the government wanted to tell them about what was happening at the battle front. In fact the government and the army accused Russell at one time of being a traitor for all the information he gave out.

Whenever a war takes place some distance away, people are only able to know what they are told, by governments, by the army, by journalists. There is always the danger that they are either not told the truth, or that they are told so little that they cannot possibly understand properly what is happening in the war.

It is as much of a danger nowadays, as it was in 1854 during the Crimean War.

See also November 5th.

Florence Nightingale

23 October

In 1952 a Frenchman named Dr Alain Bombard crossed the Atlantic alone in a rubber dinghy. He had no supplies on board, except a sealed box of emergency rations. When he landed in Barbados after 65 days at sea, the box was still untouched. He had conjured enough food and water from the ocean to keep himself not just alive, but also reasonably healthy.

Dr Bombard embarked upon his amazing journey simply to prove that it *was* possible to survive under such conditions. He was appalled at the number of deaths there were at sea – not those killed during a shipwreck, but those who died afterwards, *after* they had safely reached the lifeboats. He wrote:

'Ninety per cent of the survivors of a shipwreck die within three days, yet it takes longer than that to perish of hunger and thirst. When his ship goes down a man's whole universe goes with it. Because he no longer has a deck under his feet his courage and reason abandon him. Even if he reaches a lifeboat, he is not necessarily safe. He sits, slumped, contemplating his misery, and can hardly be said to be alive. Helpless in the night, chilled by sea and wind, terrified by the solitude, by noise, and by silence, he takes less than three days to surrender his life.'

Dr Bombard was certain that these people need not die. He believed that if people knew how to use what the sea offered them by way of food and water, they could survive, for if they had the knowledge, they could conquer their fear.

He experimented in his laboratory to find out if raw fish and plankton (minute sea creatures which float in water) were enough to provide food. Then he tried to work out whether enough water could be obtained from fish, together with small amounts of seawater, to stop a person from dying of thirst.

He proved it to himself; then he set out to prove it to the rest of the world, in his rubber dinghy *L'Hérétique*.

Here is an extract from his record of the voyage, from October 23rd onwards.

'I had hardly gathered way again when the harvest of fish began. They appeared first as green and blue stains in the water, timid to start with, and approaching the dinghy with great suspicion. They disappeared with a flip of their tails as soon as I made any sudden gesture. However, it was high time to start laying in a supply. During the whole day of the 24th I worked at bending the point of my knife, gently, without breaking it, on the flat part of an oar, as if on an anvil. I then bound the handle of the knife with a length of twine to the end of an oar so that I could harpoon the first fish which came near enough. Almost anything will serve as a lashing – a necktie, shoe laces, a belt, or strands of rope; a castaway would always have something of the sort. I intended to dispense as far as possible with my emergency fishing kit (normal equipment, in a sealed box, carried by most lifeboats) as someone on a raft might well be without it. I intended to do what I could with the material on board. While I was working away, I was astonished to see several birds, wheeling overhead. I had been convinced there would be none once I was out of range of land, and the sight of them exploded another landlubber's notion. No day was to pass without my seeing some form of bird life. One bird in particular became a personal acquaintance. Every day of the voyage, he appeared at about four o'clock, to circle a few times over *L'Hérétique*. But for the time being I was concentrating on the fish.

On Saturday 25th, I managed to catch my first dolphin. I was saved: not only did I have food and drink, but bait and hook as well. Behind the gill cover, there is a perfect natural bone hook, such as has been found in the tombs of prehistoric men, and which I think I can claim to have adapted to modern use. My first fishing line was at hand. From then on I had all the food and liquid I needed every day, and was never in danger of starving.'

He survived, and reached Barbados, proving his argument beyond doubt. He concluded:

'Any survivor of a disaster at sea should be able to reach land in as good physical condition as I did. Mine was a perfectly normal case and my health was that of the average man . . .

I claim to have proved that the sea itself provides sufficient food and drink to enable the battle for survival to be fought with perfect confidence.

During the sixty-five days it took me to get from the Canaries to the West Indies I enjoyed no particular good fortune and my voyage cannot be considered an exceptional case or a mere hazardous exploit . . .

For sixty-five days I lived exclusively on what I could catch from the sea . . .

I had no rainwater for the first twenty-three days. During the whole of that period I proved conclusively that I could quench my thirst from fish and that the sea itself provides the liquid necessary to health. After leaving Monaco, I drank sea-water for fourteen days in all and fish juice for forty-three days. I had conquered the menace of thirst at sea.'

Dr Bombard emerged from his ordeal convinced that it is people's own determination to stay alive that is the key to whether they survive or die in a lifeboat. The story of his own amazing voyage certainly shows it.

24 October

Today is United Nations Day on which we remember the efforts of people everywhere who work for greater understanding and peace throughout the world. This poem by Paul Robeson explains the feelings that guide them:

Road of Peace

Build a road of peace before us,
Build it wide and deep and long.
Speed the slow and check the eager
Help the weak and curb the strong.
None shall push beside another
None shall let another fall,
March together sister, brother,
All for one
And one for all!

October

26 October

The first telephone was made from a violin case, a hollowed-out beer-barrel bung, and a stretched sausage skin. It was demonstrated on October 26th 1861, when excited listeners heard parts of song being sung over 200 metres away in another building. The telephone was the invention of a German named Johann Reis. We don't really

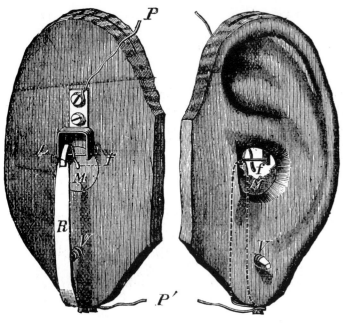

An early attempt at a telephone by Reis.

know what it sounded like. Listeners said they recognised the song, but there seems some doubt whether they were able to understand more than a few words and it is likely that they could not hear it continually, only a few words, now and then.

Fifteen years later, Alexander Graham Bell invented a telephone on which the first fully recognisable sentence was spoken. Bell was working in his attic in Boston, in America, and his assistant, Thomas Watson, was downstairs. Suddenly Watson heard Bell's voice saying, 'Mr Watson, come here, I want you.' This was the first telephone message ever sent. At that time, Bell's telephone only worked in one direction, so Mr Watson could not reply.

At almost exactly the same time, another American, named Elisha Gray had invented his own telephone. But, because Bell registered his invention officially a few hours before Gray, he is usually called the man who invented the telephone. In fact both of them developed the brilliant idea fully, quite separately from each other, and both of them used some of the ideas of the German inventor Reis.

A few months later, Bell's telephone was put on show at an exhibition in Philadelphia. Not many people paid any attention to it, until the Emperor of Brazil had a look, and exclaimed in surprise, 'My god, it talks!'

In the autumn of that year – September 7th – Bell's telephone was first shown in Glasgow, Scotland, and on July 14th of the following year, 1877, he laid the first telephone line between two buildings, in London, for a short demonstration.

At last, 16 years after that very first demonstration of the idea in Germany, Bell's telephone went on sale to the public in October of 1877.

For the first time people could actually talk to each other across a distance. Until that time they had had either to write a letter, or to send a message by electric telegraph. It had not been possible to send the sound of a voice for even the smallest distance.

What a magical invention the telephone must have seemed! Many people probably felt a bit like the Emperor of Brazil when he exclaimed, 'My god, it talks!'

26 October

Battle of Agincourt Day in England. ▶MCF.

Independence Day in Austria. ▶MCF.

A story for Divali

At this time of year, Hindus are celebrating the festival of Divali. Here is one of the stories told at this time. It has been told for thousands of years.

There was once a king Dasharatha, who ruled the northern kingdom of Ayodhya in India. He had four sons.

There came a time when King Dasharatha knew that it would not be long before he died, for he was old and tired. He called his people together and said, 'I am going to make my son Rama king after me, for he is wise, and good, and will make a just ruler. Prepare the ceremonies for his coronation.'

The people all rejoiced. They knew the kingdom would be well cared for if Rama took the throne. But Rama's stepmother was jealous. Why had her son Bharata not been chosen to be the future king? Long, long ago, the king had promised her that if she ever asked two favours of him, he would grant them to her at once.

Now, with her mind so poisoned by her jealousy and ambition for her son that it overwhelmed any other thoughts, she went and asked him to grant her two things. The first, was that Bharata should be made king. The second, that Rama should be banished from Ayodhya, and live in poverty in the forests for 14 years.

When he heard this, grief clouded the old king's face. Sorrow overwhelmed him. But he had given a promise, and he could not break his word. He asked Rama to come to him, and told him what his stepmother had asked.

With no hesitation, Rama agreed to follow all his father's wishes. He would leave the kingdom at once, and live in exile in the forest. He asked his wife, Sita, to stay in the safety of the palace. The forest would be dangerous: wild elephants and other beasts roamed there. It would be a life of great hardship and poverty.

But Sita replied, 'No danger is great enough to make me leave your side. I will come with you wherever you have to go.'

Lakshmana, Rama's other half-brother, went too, for he had vowed to protect them from the dangers of the wilds. And so the three set off, to begin their long years of banishment.

It was not very long before the old King Dasharatha died. His heart had broken with the loss of his well-loved son. And when Bharata heard of his mother's envious deeds, he was very, very angry. He loved his brother, Rama, and he knew he would be a wise, good king. Now, because of his mother's jealous schemes, he had lost both a father and a brother. Being king of Ayodhya could never replace that loss.

At once he set off into the forest, to search for Rama and to bring him back to take the throne. Rama refused. He would keep his promise to his father, and live in the forest as long as he had asked. Bharata vowed that he would rule in Rama's place for exactly 14 years, but live a simple life outside the city; on the throne he would place the golden sandals of the rightful king, Rama, as a sign to all that he would one day return to claim the throne.

Ten years passed. Rama, Sita and Lakshmana lived as they had promised. They encountered many adventures, battled against many dangers. Evil demons tried to tempt them from their simple ways. Others tried to seize them and carry them off. But they never won, for Rama and Lakshmana were victorious in every battle they fought.

There was a mighty demon, Ravana, with ten heads and 20 arms, who saw Sita and longed to have her as his bride. He devised a plan to seize her by trickery. He changed another demon into a golden deer to entice Rama from his wife's side. Lakshmana stayed, to protect her. But when the magic deer cried in the voice of Rama that he needed help, Lakshmana drew a magic circle around Sita, and told her to remain in it. Then he left her, and went to help his brother.

At once Ravana the demon appeared, disguised as a holy man. Sita suspected nothing. Trustingly, she left the circle to talk to him. Swiftly Ravana changed into his vile, many-headed form, and swept her up into the skies in his speeding demon-chariot.

In vain Rama and Lakshmana searched the forest. No trace of Sita could be found. They searched and searched. But years went by, and all their looking was in vain. At last the monkey god, Hanuman, came to their aid. He summoned all his monkey hordes – a great army to spread through all the forests and seek for Sita. Still not one of them could find her.

One day an eagle told them he had seen her flying in the chariot towards the demon's palace on Lanka, an island far off the southern coast of India. With a single bound Hanuman leapt across the ocean and crept by night into Ravana's palace. There he saw Sita, and swiftly returned to Rama, so that they could prepare a great army to cross the seas and rescue her.

To build a bridge across the sea, they tore up great boulders and trees, and threw them in the water. Then the assembled army of forest creatures crossed, and from Ravana's kingdom, Lanka, the demons rose against them. The mighty battle raged, beginning each dawn afresh, until at last Rama and Ravana fought face to face. With mighty blows Rama sliced off each of the demon's heads. But every time another grew in its place, so mighty were the demon's magic powers.

Then Rama prayed to the gods for help. They sent him a magic bow of sunlight and fire, heavy as a mountain. He strung the bow and shot his final arrow at the demon. He saw it strike, and sweep the demon from his chariot. He fell to the ground, lifeless. His army fled. The demons had been conquered.

Rama and Sita were together again at last. In triumph Hanuman sped towards Ayodhya, to give the joyful news. Bharata and the people of the kingdom polished the city till it gleamed. They hung bright streamers and flags from every tower. They lit a thousand lamps to shine through the night and guide the returning Rama to his throne.

Each year, at the festivals of Navaratri, Dusshera and Divali, Hindu people celebrate the story: they rejoice in the defeat of evil – the demon Ravana – by the power of good – Rama and his helpers, the loyal brother Lakshmana and the monkey god, Hanuman, with all his hordes of forest warriors. And they celebrate the steadfast loyalty of Sita, who despite her captivity, refused to become the demon's bride and remained true to Rama.

At Navaratri, people remember the time when Rama prepared to do battle with Ravana to rescue Sita. At Dusshera, they remember his victory over the demon; a great effigy of the demon is ceremoniously burned. And at Divali, the lamps are lit to guide victorious Rama to his home.

Note to readers

To refer you to relevant material, including songs, in other Ward Lock Educational books we have used this symbol ▶
See page 4

October

Gérard's alternating current machine

to the public and making a great deal of money in the process.

It was more than forty years before electric lamps for sale to the public were developed. Inventors in England and America worked out how to make them at about the same time, in the late 1870s.

But the changeover from gas lighting to electric lighting was not as fast as might have been expected. Even as little as 60 years ago, 40 years after they had gone on sale, only about 12 in every 100 homes in Britain had electric lighting. In another 17 years, a little more than half the homes in Britain had it. It was only about 24 years ago that the number rose to as many as 96 in every 100 homes.

31 October

Hallowe'en. *See* Class Assemblies on page 114. ▶ MCF.

30 October

Nowadays, we can put on a light with the flick of a switch. It is rather difficult to imagine how fascinating it must have seemed the first time anyone succeeded in doing this. All other kinds of lighting needed to be lit with a flame – gas and oil lamps, for example. And oil lamps also had to be filled with oil.

By contrast, the light given out by an electric lamp seemed almost magical. Here's how a journalist described it,

'In beauty the light surpasses all others, has no smell, emits no smoke, is incapable of explosion, and not requiring air for combustion can be kept in sealed jars. It ignites without the aid of a taper . . .

It may be sent to any convenient distance, and the apparatus for producing it is contained in a common chest.'

This is, in fact, a description of the first ever electric lamp, which was invented by a Scottish scientist, James Bowman Lindsay. On October 30th 1835, he wrote to a Scottish newspaper describing how he had used a glass tube without air in it to make the lamp; and people were very impressed when they realised that the letter had been written by the light of the lamp, thus proving that it really had worked. But, having so successfully made electric light, James Bowman simply moved on to experiment with other things, he was not at all interested in putting the invention on sale

In some years the following festivals may fall in November:

Divali (Hindu festival) *see* page 30. ▶F&F.

Meelad ul-Nabi, celebration of Prophet Muhammad's birthday, *see* page 38.

1 November

Portugal, 220 years ago today. The city of Lisbon on All Saints' Day. The people of the city are all in church, lighting candles, praying.

Suddenly, a trembling in the ground. A deep, threatening rumble from the earth. Buildings shake, begin to totter ... 'the whole city waving backwards and forwards like the sea'.

And with a shudder, the city's buildings crumble to the ground. Waves seven metres high surge up the River Tagus into the city. Quaysides disappear beneath the water, swallowed by gigantic cracks in the seabed.

Many thousands of people lost their lives that day in Lisbon, for the city was totally destroyed. Many more died across the sea in North Africa, which was also hit by the earthquake. Even 5600 kilometres away, waves thrown up by the tremors battered the beaches of the West Indies on the other side of the Atlantic Ocean.

This appalling disaster made some scientists determined to prevent people from suffering such death and destruction again. They tried to learn as much as they could about earthquakes. In particular, the Portuguese asked scientists from all over the world to send them information about earth tremors in their own countries at the time of the Lisbon disaster.

After that, the study of earthquakes developed a great deal, and we now understand a lot more about them.

Nowadays, buildings in areas which suffer frequent earthquakes have to be constructed in a special way. And scientists have developed instruments which can measure earthquake shocks, working out where they will travel across the earth. Because of this, it is now possible to warn people, and give them time to escape before an earthquake strikes.

See also July page 107.

2 November

In 1936 John Logie Baird and the BBC opened the world's first regular public television service, sent out from Alexandra Palace, North London. *See* January 27th.

All Souls' Day, a Christian day dedicated to the souls of the dead. ▶MCF.

Jewish National Home Day, marking the 1917 Balfour declaration in favour of a homeland for Jews. ▶MCF.

5 November

On this day in 1854, Florence Nightingale and 38 other nurses arrived at a large hospital in Scutari, Turkey. They found a stinking, rat-and lice-infested building; a swamp of mud, rotting rubbish and half-buried bodies of dead animals in the courtyard. Filth from blocked drains and sewers seeped everywhere, and a poisonous stench filled the air. Dead and dying British soldiers lay around, many waiting days before anyone could tend to them, for there were so few doctors and each one was overworked.

The doctors had no equipment of any kind – no medicines, no furniture, not even a table for doing operations. Nor was there a screen to hide the operations from other patients waiting to have one themselves.

There were none of the simple necessities either – clothes for the wounded who had been carried from the battlefield in bloody, tattered clothes. Nothing for them to eat with – neither plates nor knives and forks. There were no pillows, blankets, mattresses ... It was hardly surprising that more than a third of the wounded died in the hospital.

At the time, Britain, France and Turkey were at war with Russia, fighting on a penisular in the Black Sea called the Crimea. The wounded from these battles were brought to this hospital where Florence Nightingale and her nurses now prepared to care for them.

They got to work, by their efforts transforming the hospital. The government was forced to investigate the rotten drains, provide new ones, supply clean water. They had even discovered that the water supply was flowing through the dead body of a horse!

Equipment and medicines began to reach them. As Florence Nightingale and her team of nurses began to tend and care for the sick, the number of soldiers dying in the hospital began to drop. Instead of 40 out of every 100 dying now only two in every 100 died.

Yet, like many who saw for themselves the terrible misery of the soldiers in the Crimean War, Florence Nightingale remained very bitter about it. She thought of the soldiers as her children and she wrote, years later, 'I have had to see my children dressed in a dirty blanket and an old pair of regimental trousers, to see them fed off raw salted meat, and nine thousand of my children are lying, from causes which might have been prevented, in their forgotten graves.'

After returning from the war, she began the first real training programme for nurses at St Thomas' hospital in London. Within 40 years she had transformed the care of sick people in hospital. Before

November

she began, nurses had been little more than minders of the patients. They were untrained, usually dirty, and often drunkards. After Florence Nightingale began her training schemes, they became skilled, efficient, knowledgeable, able to work properly alongside doctors.

There is another nurse whose name you will seldom hear mentioned in accounts of the Crimean War, but whose dedicated work earned her deep gratitude from all the British soldiers at the time. She was a Jamaican nurse, Mary Seacole. For many years she tended the victims of diseases such as cholera and yellow fever in Central America and the Caribbean, and she had invented a medicine for treating cholera.

When she heard of the Crimean War and the work of Florence Nightingale there, she travelled at once to London. There at the War Office, she offered her services as a nurse. Because of her colour, they turned her offer down.

But Mary Seacole was a determined and dedicated woman. Not at all put off by the War Office's stupidity, she travelled 3000 miles to the Crimea, to see what help she could give.

As she had not been given permission to nurse, she opened a hotel instead, and began to tend the sick and wounded there. It very quickly became a proper hospital, and as it was situated not on the mainland, like the Scutari hospital, but on the wartorn Crimean peninsular, battles often raged around the hotel.

She never ceased her work. And if the War Office had not seen it, the soldiers she saved were certainly witnesses to her selfless bravery and dedication. She used up all her money in her work during the war. The soldiers decided to help her by holding a festival of music in which more than 1000 performers, nine military bands and an orchestra, played in London, to raise money.

She was later awarded two medals for her work in the Crimea.

See also October page 27.

5 November
Guy Fawkes Night, British bonfire festival commemorating the plot to blow up the King and Parliament in 1605. ▶MCF.

7 November
There was once a quiet, shy, Polish woman who was determined to study and learn as much as she could. This doesn't sound very unusual nowadays. But at the time she lived, and particularly in Poland where she grew up, it was both very unusual and almost impossible for women to study. She was very determined. She saved and saved until she had enough money to leave Poland and go to France to study in the university in Paris.

Twelve years later, on this day in 1911, she won one of the most important international prizes for science, the Nobel Prize. Eight years after that, she won it again.

The woman was Marie Curie, and she was the first scientist ever to win two Nobel Prizes for science.

She was a remarkable person in many ways. At that time there were only a few men doing the kind of work she did. Many people were against women doing it and made it very difficult for them. Some people thought it wrong for women to do that kind of work; others thought they would be stupid and inefficient at it, and not do it anything like as well as men.

Marie Curie proved them all wrong. She showed not only that women could work alongside men as their equals, but that women could be among the best. She herself was one of the most brilliant scientists of her day.

We have much to remember Marie Curie for.

She was given the Nobel Prize for her work on radioactivity. This is a very important part of science, and is used in the treatment of disease, and in farming and industry.

Until the end of the last century, no one knew about radioactivity, or what caused it. When, at the beginning of this century, Marie and her husband Pierre discovered a new metal, radium, the study of radioactivity made an enormous leap forward. Radium was very radioactive, over a million times more so than uranium – the metal which scientists had been studying up till then. With Marie and Pierre's radium, they were able to speed up their discoveries about ways of using and controlling radioactivity. So the Curies' work was one of the foundations of the scientific knowledge of this century.

It took them four years of hard, back-breaking work to get radium. It was like looking for one *particular* grain of sugar in a whole bag with millions and millions of grains in it. They boiled up great cauldrons of a rock called pitchblende; stirred them with iron bars almost as tall as Marie herself. From each cauldron they would get a thimbleful of precious radium.

Both Marie and Pierre suffered terribly from their work. In 1934 Marie died because she had spent her life handling radioactive materials without protecting herself from them. Nowadays we know about the deadly radiation sickness. We know that people should wear special clothing and never touch a radioactive substance. In Marie and Pierre's time, a lot less was known about it, and many early workers suffered and died as a result.

But the young scientists whom Marie trained developed a great knowledge about the effects of radioactivity and about how to use and control it. This knowledge is now applied in all the areas of life where radioactivity is used. Radium itself is one of the most important weapons in treating cancer, and radiation, which killed Marie, is now used to treat many diseases.

7 November

National Day in the Ukraine. ▶MCF.

11 November

Today is Remembrance Day, a day on which we remember all those who died in the First and Second World Wars. November 11th was chosen because it was the day on which the First World War came to an end.

Thus finished four long years in which armies had lived, and fought and died in muddy trenches in northern France and Belgium. Desperately, and violently, they fought to win a few yards of marshy ground, and then lost it again, while millions of soldiers died.

During that time a Canadian doctor wrote a poem about the poppies which bloomed across the battlefields and between the graves; it was published in Britain in Punch Magazine in 1915. At the time people in Britain said that the poppy bloomed on those dismal fields because it grew on the blood of the slaughtered. And so this blood-red flower came to stand for everything that was tragic and pointless about the loss of lives in that grim war.

From that time on the poppy has been used to remind us of the tragedy of war. An organisation decided to make and sell imitation poppies to raise money for crippled and shell-shocked soldiers and their families. This poppy appeal continues every year to this day.

Here is another poem written about those fields in Flanders where so many died:

Last year the fields were all glad and gay
With silver daisies and silver may;
There were kingcups gold by the river's edge
And primrose stars under every hedge.

This year the fields are trampled and brown,
The hedges are broken and beaten down,
And where the primroses used to grow
Are little black crosses set in a row.

And the flower of hopes, and the flowers of
    dreams,
The noble, fruitful, beautiful schemes,
The tree of life with its fruit and bud,
Are trampled down in the mud and the
    blood.

The changing seasons will bring again
The magic of Spring to our wood and plain:
Though the Spring be so green as never was
    seen
The crosses will still be black in the green.

The Fields of Flanders Edith Nesbit

15 November

There was a time when a patient having an operation in hospital would have had either to be tied down, or held down by two strong assistants. Sometimes the patients tried to escape in the middle of an operation, staggering in terror away from the surgeon who was forced to chase them in order to finish his work.

These things happened because at the time there was no way of putting a patient to sleep during the operation, and no other way of killing the pain.

Surgeons could shorten a patient's agony only by doing the operation at top speed. Most of them

November

took somewhere between 54 seconds and a minute. (Compare that with the many hours of careful work done by a modern surgeon!) Because of the speed necessary, there were not many kinds of operations that could be done.

One surgeon practised shaving with his left hand, and sharpened pencils by the hundreds, just so that he could train his fingers to work faster.

However there were a number of doctors in Britain and America who were searching for ways of putting patients to sleep. In America, a chemical called ether had been used successfully by a dentist. But it smelled very unpleasant, and it made some people very sick.

Then one day in 1847 Dr James Simpson brought two of his assistants home for dinner in Edinburgh. After dinner he asked that he and his guests be left alone for a while. Someone listening in the next room heard their conversation become more and more loud. Then there was a thud, and silence. In the dining room the three men had slipped from their chairs and were sprawled unconscious on the floor.

When they woke up, they were none the worse for their experience. But they had performed a very important experiment. They had sniffed a chemical called chloroform, and it had swiftly and peacefully put them to sleep.

Within a fortnight, Dr Simpson had tried out chloroform successfully on 50 patients, including a woman giving birth to a child.

But, as with all new developments, people were a bit suspicious of it. It wasn't until Queen Victoria used it for the birth of her eighth child, and said that she found it 'soothing, quieting and delightful beyond measure', that it started to be used widely by doctors.

Its effects were enormous. Because it reduced the pain and suffering of patients, a lot fewer died of

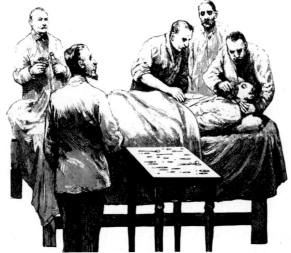

shock. Because their patients suffered less, surgeons were able to work more slowly and carefully and more and more difficult operations could be done.

So began, about 140 years ago, what is known as anaesthetics; and nowadays no one would dream of having even the smallest kind of operation (like a tooth out) without some form of anaesthetic to kill the pain.

21 November

The first creatures to travel by air were a sheep, a duck and a cock. They went up in a balloon and were watched by the king of France himself. Later that same year, at 1.45pm on November 21st, 1783, the first men to fly rose into the air.

They took off their hats and bowed to the assembled crowd of spectators below, which included the king's eldest son and all his courtiers. Then upwards they soared 900 metres into the air, and wafted across the city of Paris, sinking to the ground again eight kilometres away.

The two intrepid flyers were Frenchmen – a young science professor, Pilatre de Rozier, and the Marquis Francois d'Arlandes. Their craft was a balloon made from cane covered with paper-lined linen. A fire, suspended in a container underneath, made hot air, which made the balloon rise into the air. The passengers travelled in a ring-shaped basket below the balloon, like a narrow gallery encircling the fire.

Throughout the flight they tossed straw on the fire to keep it going. It was a dangerous task. Several times the covering of the balloon went up in flames and they had to put them out with water-soaked sponges.

It was only six months since the first balloon had ever sailed through the air. Like the one in which de Rozier and d'Arlande travelled, it was made by the Montgolfier brothers. They had been experimenting for some time. At first they tried burning old shoes and bad meat to make the gas. In the end they found that damp straw and wool made the best mixture.

Their successful balloon journeys started a craze for 'ballooning' which swept across France and Europe. Different people competed with each other to do the most inventive and daring flight. A professor named Jacques Charles launched a balloon filled with a gas called hydrogen.

De Rozier himself made a number of other successful flights in the following year. In the end, however, he was killed while making a daring attempt to cross the Channel from France to England in a double balloon, made up of a Montgolfier fire balloon and Professor Charles' hydrogen-filled one. Unfortunately for De Rozier, it blew up.

22 November

Independence Day in Lebanon. ▶MCF.

The story of rain

This is a very ancient story from Australia. It tells of the importance of rain in a land where there is little water.

In the spirit land there was a spirit god, and the spirit god was lord of all – he who must not be angered, he whose power reigned above all else.

But there came a time when someone spoke against him, dared to challenge his power. It was none other than the god's own son, Tjinim, who risked his father's fury. Then the spirit lord's anger flamed, bitter and vengeful against his son. In rage he flew towards him and prepared to hurl his punishment upon him.

Tjinim fled. He tried to reach beyond the spirit river which carved the boundary between the spirit land and earth. But he could not. The god caught him and raised his club to strike him down. They locked in desperate combat, each fighting for his very life; and the spirit world around them thundered to the fury of the battle sounds.

Then Tjinim seized a spear and drove it with all his strength into the body of the spirit god.

Down fell the god. In agony he writhed and twisted where he lay. He dragged himself towards the cooling waters of the spirit river, there to soothe his wounds. But the searing burn of pain was everywhere, and writhing, twisting with the torment of it, he became the coiling body of a gigantic snake.

Into the river he fell, and in a torrent of water, he crashed beyond, downward to the earth below, the spirit water gushing and splashing downwards from the heavens with him.

The earth was flat and formless. Nothing lived on it. But in his falling the great snake gouged a crater from the land. And there the spirit waters gathered, swelled, became the first lake on the earth . . .

To and fro he dragged his painful body, carving deep valleys in the land. Mountains and hills rose up on either side of his thrashing, form. All the while the spirit waters flowed, gathered in the hollows so that streams and rivers now criss-crossed the once-dry land. .

Gradually the life-giving moisture caused new stirrings in the earth. Plants pushed their shoots above the soil. Flowers unfolded blooms. Insects, animals, birds . . . everywhere there was movement, colour, life awakening.

In the snake's enormous body all the colours gleamed, shone – as though he was a great mirror to the life that swelled . . . And now his torment lessened. Wounds healed, pain faded. His strength returned.

Until one day he had the power to make his leap up beyond the clouds into his spirit world again. And so he leapt, and left behind him, hanging in the sky, his many-coloured snake-skin, arching above the bright new world.

And so was born the rainbow in the sky.

The elephant we remember

Have you ever wondered why large things – big elephants and enormous aeroplanes, for example – are called Jumbo?

They are named after an African elephant who became very famous at London Zoo in its early years last century.

He was enormous – well over three metres tall, weighing six and a half tonnes. He and his keeper began the tradition of giving children rides, but in time he became very bad tempered. The zoo decided to sell him to an American circus. The British people were appalled. Sell Jumbo!

Questions were asked in the House of Commons! A 'Save Jumbo for the Nation' Fund was started. Jumbo songs and Jumbo cartoons appeared. The *Daily Telegraph* newspaper even sent a telegram which said: 'Editor's compliments. All British children distressed at elephant's departure. Hundreds of correspondents beg to enquire on what terms you will kindly return Jumbo.'

Despite all this, Jumbo and his keeper sailed for America.

These were the early days at the zoo, and the animals arrived in quite exotic ways, causing quite a stir amongst the crowds who gathered to watch them pass. The first chimpanzee, Tommy, travelled in a stagecoach from Bristol to London. The first giraffes arrived by ship and then had to walk to the zoo from the London Docks, causing amazement amongst the crowds, who'd never seen such a sight before.

Obaysch, the first hippopotamus, was just a baby when he sailed down the Nile in a barge specially built for him, complete with his own private herd of goats to provide him with milk on the journey. People were quite taken by this extraordinary animal. One visitor said, 'I have seen the hippo asleep and awake, and I can assure you that he is the ugliest of the works of God.'

Guru Nanak's birthday

Today the Sikhs are celebrating the birthday of the founder of the Sikh religion, Guru Nanak. It is a time when his life and teachings are remembered.

Here is one story about his early life, when he was still quite young, and had not yet begun the Sikh religion. He was, however, already thinking deeply about the world, trying to understand people's hopes and fears, to understand the world of Nature and the ways of God.

His father was a wealthy government official who hoped to teach his son to become a successful and wealthy businessman.

November

One day, he gave Guru Nanak a sum of money. 'Go to the city,' he said 'With this money, I want you to buy some goods that we can sell again to make a lot of money. Buy well; that is, buy cheaply, so that we can sell at a price which will bring us in a good profit.' And off he sent him, hoping his son would learn his business lesson well.

Guru Nanak had not travelled very far, when he met a group of holy men wandering the countryside, depending on the generosity of others to give them food and drink. At once he saw how weak and pale they looked, how frail their bodies. He realised that they were starving for lack of food. Without hesitation, he held the money out to them, urging them to take it and buy food.

'We cannot,' the holy men replied. 'It is against our beliefs to take money from anyone. We *can* accept food from you.'

Guru Nanak turned and travelled as fast as he could to the nearest town. There he spent all the money buying food, then carried it back and served it himself to the holy men. They ate thankfully, with pleasure at Guru Nanak's generosity.

This money, thought Guru Nanak, has truly turned into a great profit, for it has taken away the pain and hunger of these holy men. And he turned for home, well pleased with his expedition.

Of course his father was not so pleased!

Prophet Muhammad's birthday

On Meelad ul-Nabi, the birthday of the Prophet Muhammad, many stories are told about his life. Here is one tale, of a journey through the seven heavens of creation and into the presence of God himself.

Muhammad woke, suddenly. It was just before dawn.

'Arise,' a voice had said to him. 'Muhammad arise. Come with me, for the time has come.'

He rose from his bed, and there before him was the Angel Gabriel. He beckoned, and led Muhammad from the house into the garden. There, agleam in the darkness, there was a horse – a giant, the great white mare Burraq – her face a human face; her four hooves arching from the horizon in the west to the horizon in the east; her wings spanned wide across the earth. In an instant, Muhammad was astride her and rising into the sky, Mecca and his home left far behind.

In no more than a moment's thought they had flown a great distance and were already at Jerusalem. There, in the mosque, Muhammad saw all the prophets who had gone before him, the great teachers of many ages and of many lands. They met in prayer, together.

Then out into the night Gabriel led him once again. A ladder of light rose from the earth, soared upwards to the heavens. Muhammad climbed, and began his journey through the seven heavens. In each he saw such splendour he had never seen before. And all the teachers of the past were there to greet him – Adam and Noah, John the Baptist and Aaron, brother of Moses. He saw the Angel of Death, and the Angel of Tears, and the angel who guards heaven and earth . . .

At last he passed beyond. He was in a place where fragrance filled the air. A mood of warmth and love took hold of him. He felt the gentle touch of an invisible hand which brought him indescribable joy and peace, and he knew that he now stood before God himself.

He spoke with God and received great wisdom from him, great knowledge, to take back to earth and give to people there.

Then down he journeyed once again, descending the ladder of light. Through the sky he flew on Burraq, and reached his home. It was still just before dawn. Descending from the miraculous mare, he saw now that his journey into heaven, all the wonders he had seen and heard and felt, had taken no more than it would take him just to think it – minutes – almost no time at all.

30 November

Today is St Andrew's Day, the feast day of the patron saint of Scotland. He was one of the first of the fishermen on the Sea of Galilee who followed Jesus Christ.

After Jesus's death, St Andrew is said to have travelled to Russia and Greece, teaching people about the Christian religion. In Greece he was captured and sentenced to death for being a Christian.

Legend tells that his body was taken to Constantinople and it was from there, 500 years later, that it began its journey to Scotland. Monks setting out to teach the Scots about Christianity carried Andrew's body with them, to give them protection on the journey.

Later, not only Scotland, but also Greece and Russia chose him as their patron saint. He is said to have been crucified on an X-shaped cross, because he believed he was unfit to die in the same way as Jesus. The Scottish flag is a white cross on a blue background – to represent the cross of St Andrew and the blue waters in which he fished.

Scottish people often celebrate on St Andrew's night, and one tradition is to carry in a haggis – a traditional dish made of sheep's stomach filled with seasoned meats, suet and oatmeal – accompanied by the music of bagpipes.

Fourth Thursday in November

Thanksgiving Day in America. ▶ MCF.

Start of Advent

On the first Sunday which is four Sundays away from Christmas, Advent begins.

Hanukkah (Chanucah) the Jewish festival falls in December. ▶ F&F and MCF.

1 December

On this day in 1955, an elderly woman named Rosa Parks got onto a bus in the southern state of Alabama, America. She found an empty seat, and sat down, thankfully, for she was going home from work, and it had been a long, hard day.

But she was not allowed to sit for long. Before the bus had gone more than a few streets, the conductor ordered her to stand at the back. The reason? Simply, that she was black, and a white American who had just entered the bus wanted her seat.

At that time, the laws of Alabama said that the white American had a right to that seat, but that the black American, Rosa Parks, did not.

Rosa was tired. Her feet hurt. The conductor's demand was not at all unusual – it had happened before. She, and others, had reluctantly obeyed. But this time, she had had enough.

She refused to move. Again the bus conductor ordered her to do so. Quietly, she refused again. Angry now, the conductor called the police, and elderly, tired Rosa was taken to the city prison.

Within hours, news of her arrest had spread among the black people of the city. Here was one more example of the injustices they had suffered all their lives. At that time in Alabama, as in other southern states of America, black and white people had very different rights. Black children had to go to different schools from the white children. The black schools were far worse. Not only on buses, but also trains, houses, restaurants, hospitals, even the prisons, black and white had to be separate.

Like Rosa Parks, other black people in the city had also had enough. When they heard of her arrest, a city-wide protest grew. Until the bus laws were changed, not one of them would take a city bus.

For 381 days, in their tens of thousands, they walked to work. And then, no matter how far they had to go, or how tired they were, back they walked again at the end of the day.

In the end, the highest law court in America judged that the laws were wrong. From then on, black and white had to be treated exactly the same on Alabama's buses.

In the months and years that followed, there were similar protests in many other southern states. Important changes were won, such as new laws forbidding the kinds of rules which Rosa Parks had so bravely refused to obey.

Hard work on the land

Those of us who only ever see food as it appears in shops or on market stalls, probably don't realise how much work is done on the land, and how many people labour for every vegetable or fruit, for every slice of bread or bowl of cereal we eat.

On farms in some countries (Britain is one of them) a great deal of farmwork is now done by machines which cost a lot of money. On other farms, in Europe, America, Africa and Asia, a lot of machinery is also used. But there are also some farms, on all these continents, where very little machinery is used, and often none at all.

Here is a description of winter farm work as it used to be in Britain. Machinery is being used alongside horsedrawn equipment. You can nowadays see people working on farms like this in some parts of Europe, while only a short distance away expensive machinery is being used. Often whether or not a farm has much machinery just depends on whether it earns enough from the crops for the farmer to afford machines.

'Very early in the morning, before daybreak for the greater part of the year, the hamlet men would throw on their clothes, breakfast on bread and lard, snatch the dinner-baskets which had been packed for them overnight, and hurry off across fields and over stiles to the farm. Getting the boys off was a more difficult matter. Mothers would have to call and shake and sometimes pull boys of eleven or twelve out of their warm beds on a winter morning. Then boots which had been drying inside the fender all night and had become shrunk and hard as boards in the process would have to be coaxed over chilblains . . .

When the men and boys from the hamlet reached the farmyard in the morning, the carter and his assistant had been at work for an hour, feeding and getting ready the horses. After giving any help required, the men and boys would harness and lead out their teams and file off to the field where their day's work was to be done.

If it rained, they donned sacks, split up one side to form a hood and cloak combined. If it was frosty, they blew upon their nails and thumped their arms across their chest to warm them. If they felt hungry after their bread-and-lard breakfast, they would pare a turnip and munch it, or try a bite or two of the rich, dark brown oilcake provided for the cattle . . .

With 'Gee!' and 'Wert up!' and 'Who-a-a, now!' the teams would draw out. The boys were hoisted to the back of the tall carthorses, and the men, walking alongside, filled their clay pipes with shag and drew the first precious puffs of the day, as, with cracking whips, clopping of hooves and jingling of harness, the teams went tramping along the muddy byways . . .

December

There were usually three or four ploughs to a field, each of them drawn by a team of three horses, with a boy at the head of the leader and the ploughman behind at the shafts. All day, up and down they would go, ribbing the pale stubble with stripes of dark furrows, which, as the day advanced, would get wider and nearer together, until at length, the whole field lay a rich velvety plum-colour.

After the plough had done its part, the horse-drawn roller was used to break down the clods; then the harrow to comb out and leave the weeds in neat piles. Then seed was sown, crops were thinned out and hoed and, in time, mown, and the whole process began again.

Machinery was just coming into use on the land. Every autumn appeared a pair of large traction engines, which, posted one on each side of a field, drew a plough across and across by means of a cable. These toured the district under their own steam for hire on the different farms . . .

Such machinery as the farmer owned was horse-drawn and was only in partial use. In some fields a horse-drawn drill would sow the seed in rows, in others a human sower would walk up and down with a basket suspended from his neck and fling the seed with both hands broadcast . . .

The labourers worked hard and well when they considered the occasion demanded it and kept up a good steady pace at all times. Some were better workmen than others, of course; but the majority took a pride in their craft and were fond of explaining to an outsider that field work was not the fool's job that some townsmen considered it. Things must be done just so and at the exact moment, they said; there were ins and outs in good land work which took a man's lifetime to learn . . .

While the ploughmen were in charge of the teams, other men went singly, or in twos or threes,

to hoe, harrow, or spread manure in other fields; others cleared ditches and saw to drains, or sawed wood or cut chaff or did other odd jobs about the farmstead. Two or three highly skilled middle-aged men were sometimes put upon piecework, hedging and ditching, sheep-shearing, thatching, or mowing, according to the season. The carter, shepherd, stockman, and blacksmith had each his own specialised job.'

Lark Rise to Candleford, Flora Thompson

12 December

Just over 80 years ago, around the turn of the century, most scientists said it would be impossible to send a radio signal across the world. They were convinced that the curve of the earth would send the sound waves shooting far out into space.

But, on this day in 1901, they were proved wrong. Guglielmo Marconi, a young Italian inventor, succeeded in sending a radio signal 3200 kilometres across the Atlantic Ocean, from Poldhu in Cornwall, England, to St John's in Newfoundland, Canada.

Ever since, the Americans have called this day 'Marconi Day', to mark his tremendous achievement. It was the beginning of many new and important developments, not least of which was the radio and television broadcasting which we now take so much for granted.

It had all begun only seven years before, in 1894. Marconi was only 20 years old. He had been reading about experiments by scientists who had sent electrical waves a short distance through the air – a matter of a metre or so. At once Marconi began to wonder if it would be possible to send not just electrical waves, but actual messages, in Morse Code. What an invention that would be! For the first time it would not be necessary to have electrical cables along which the message travelled, as in the cable telegraph then in use.

And if you didn't need cables, how easy it would be to send it across seas, the oceans, across the whole world!

Without further delay, he set to work, experimenting in the attics of his home in Italy. It was not long before he had sent a radio signal from one attic to another – a distance of ten metres. The next step was to try a longer distance. So he attempted sending from one chestnut tree in his garden to another, just under 2 kilometres away. Even more amazing, a hill in between did not seem to interfere at all.

Now Marconi was certain that he was on to something very important – a system of sending messages that came to be known as the wireless, simply because it did not have wires. We usually call it the radio these days.

He was particularly determined to send a wireless signal across water. By this time he was living in Britain, and he continued his work there. In 1897, only three years after his very first experiments, he succeeded in sending a signal for a distance of over five kilometres across the Bristol Channel. So began one of the most important parts of Marconi's invention for the world at that time.

If the wireless could send messages across the water, then ships could use it. In 1899, the full importance of this was proved when the wireless was used for the first time to save lives on a distressed ship. The *Elbe* was stranded on a sandbank. She sent out a wireless call for help, and every one of her crew were saved.

At this time, ships usually only communicated with the land (or with each other) if they were within the range of the human eye or ear so that rockets or flags could be used. If they were further away than this, no one would know what was happening on board, and the ship could not contact anyone else.

It was only Marconi's wireless that changed this. If it had a wireless, a ship could hear the weather news. If it developed problems, it could send for help. If it heard another call for help, it could go to the aid of the other ship.

There was great excitement when the first ocean newspaper was produced – *The Transatlantic Times*. Here is what the first issue said:

'Through the courtesy of Mr G Marconi, the passengers on board the St Paul are accorded a rare privilege, that of receiving news several hours before landing. Mr Marconi and his assistant have arranged to work the apparatus used in reporting the Yacht Race in New York, and are now receiving despatches from their station at the Needles. War news from South Africa and home messages from London and Paris are being received . . . As all know, this is the first time that such a venture as this has been undertaken. A newspaper published at sea and Wireless Telegraph messages received and printed on a ship going twenty knots an hour!'

But the world really began to understand how important wireless was to ships at sea when the enormous luxury steamer, *The Titanic* hit an iceberg in mid-Atlantic and sank on her first voyage. Although many lives were lost, only the wireless prevented everybody on board from being drowned.

See April 14th and 15th.

13 December

Many towns and cities in this country are now preparing to switch on electric Christmas lights and decorations. It is interesting to realise that it was just a little over 100 years ago today, in 1878, that the first electric streetlighting in Britain was turned on.

It was on the Victoria Embankment, in London, and people were extremely impressed with it. They commented on how it banished the shadows which had always lurked around the lamp-posts and odd corners of gas-lit streets and made them murky and quite frightening.

The first street ever to be lit by electricity was actually in Lyons in France, 21 years before. But the French did not go any further with it until June 1878, when they installed electric lights in the 'avenue of the opera' in Paris.

Such was the impression of brightness and beauty, that the London authorities at once asked the French to install lights on the Victoria Embankment. By December 13th they were ready to be ceremoniously switched on, in time for the Christmas season.

Note to readers

To refer you to relevant material, including songs, in other Ward Lock Educational books we have used this symbol ▶
See page 4

December

14 December

On this day in 1911, the Norwegian explorer Roald Amundsen and four companions reached the South Pole – the 'bottom of the world'. They were the first men ever to get there.

They had been preparing for over a year, living in that great region of ice and snow. First they had to set up supply depots – that is, food, fuel and other essential supplies – which they left at intervals along the route they would travel to the Pole. This meant that they did not have to carry everything with them. Then equipment had to be checked and rechecked, and carefully packed. They had to wait for the beginning of the brief Antarctic spring, when the weather would be milder.

They first started out on September 8th. But the weather swiftly turned bitter against them, and Amundsen decided they should return to base.

On October 19th, 1911, they started out again: five men, with four sledges each drawn by fourteen dogs. This time the weather stayed mild, and they managed to travel reasonably fast, reaching each of the supply depots in turn and picking up food and fuel in good time. Then they were into unknown territory. And now the weather turned. They battled through freezing temperatures, up steep glaciers, across thin bridges of ice between huge crevasses which could swallow men, dogs and sledges in an instant.

But fifty-six days later, they reached the Pole. They had won the race to get there, beating the English explorers, Robert Scott and his team, by 35 days.

Just over a month later Amundsen and his companions reached their home camp again, exhausted and in severe pain from frostbite, but alive and rejoicing in their tremendous success. And five days later they sailed away from that great land of ice and snow where they had lived for over a year.

They knew nothing of the tragic struggle for survival which was then taking place as the gallant British team led by Robert Scott began their journey 1,280 kilometres back to their base camp from the South Pole.

They had reached the Pole on January 17th, when Amundsen and his companions were already well on their way back to their home camp. Their journey there had been a hard one. Vicious weather, and terrible conditions underfoot had made their progress slow and difficult. At first the snow was like soft sand into which they sank, having great difficulty pulling their single, heavily-laden sledge. Then they encountered deep ridges of snow frozen into waves which made travelling even worse, and which ripped at their ankles as they stumbled across it.

When they reached the Pole, these five, fit, healthy men were already exhausted. And now as they turned for home, the weather worsening, the hardships of the outward journey began to take their toll. One by one they sickened. Eyes became painful, hand and faces became frostbitten. They had falls which caused painful injuries and made moving slow and difficult.

Then, to their horror they found that the oil supplies in the last few depots had evaporated away. They had almost no fuel to keep them warm or cook hot meals. This above all, sapped their failing strength and made the battle for survival one which they could not win.

On February 4th, Scott and Evans, another member of the team, fell into a deep crevasse. Scott was not badly hurt, but Evans injured his head. 13 days later, he died from that fall. He was the first of them to go.

The second, Captain Oates, believed that he was slowing his companions down and risking their deaths. In one of those gestures which has gone down in history as an act of great heroism and courage, he walked out into a blizzard, making clear to the others that he did not want to be followed. He never returned.

The three survivors, Bowers, Wilson and Scott, struggled on. Scott wrote in his diary, knowing they were going to die: 'Had we lived, I would have had a tale to tell of the hardihood, endurance, and courage of my companions which would have stirred the heart of every Englishman. These rough notes and our dead bodies must tell the tale.'

By March 21st it was over two months since they had started for home. The blizzards were now so bad that they could move no further. They curled up in their sleeping bags and waited for what they knew would be their fate. A week went by. Just before the end, Scott wrote: 'Since the 21st we have had a continuous gale from W.S.W and S.W. We had fuel to make two cups of tea apiece and bare food for two days on the 20th. Every day we have been ready to start for our depot *11 miles* away, but outside the door of the tent it remains a scene of whirling drift. I do not think we can hope for any better things now. We shall stick it out to the end, but we are getting weaker, of course, and the end cannot be far . . . It seems a pity, but I do not think I can write more . . . For God's sake look after our people.'

And so the challenge of exploration and discovery took a tragic toll. On the one hand, people had seen a region never before reached. Even on their homeward journey Scott and his team collected rock specimens which were found with them when their bodies were discovered many months later. Because of this, a great deal was learned about the history of the Antarctic.

But on the other hand, there were the bitter, painful deaths of five gallant and brave men, whose determined battle against the murderous temperatures and blizzards of the Antarctic was doomed almost from the start.

See also July 22nd.

Birthday of Guru Gobind Singh

At this time, when Sikhs are celebrating the birthday of their teacher Guru Gobind Singh, one of the stories remembered is how he formed the Sikh brotherhood, the Khalsa, many centuries ago. This is also remembered at the Sikh New Year, Baisakhi, (April 13th) for it was at this festival in 1699, that Guru Gobind Singh called the Sikhs to him. He had decided that it was time for all Sikhs to declare their loyalty and faith in their religion, and their preparedness to defend it.

He stood before the doorway of a tent, facing the assembled crowd.

'Is there any one among you willing to lay down your life for your faith?' he asked.

In silence, the crowd stared at him. They moved uneasily, and for long moments no-one answered him.

Then, at last, a man stepped forward. The Guru took him inside the tent. A minute passed and Guru Gobind Singh appeared in the doorway again. In his hand, the sword dripped blood.

The crowd gasped in shock, and fearfully stepped back. But again the Guru asked, 'Is there any one among you willing to lay down your life for your faith?'

There was another reluctant pause. Then again a volunteer stepped forward. The Guru went into the tent with him, and returned, his sword bloody, as before.

Three more times he asked his question. Three more men stepped forward to meet their deaths.

The crowd grew more restless, wondering how many times the Guru would seek to test their faith.

After the fifth killing, the Guru reappeared. With him were the five volunteers for death.

Every one was alive, and quite unharmed. Five goats had met their deaths instead. But the men's courage in going to their deaths was an example to all the others there, showing the strength of will, and loyalty needed to defend their faith.

Then Guru Gobind Singh made a drink of sugar crystals and water. He sprinkled some on the fire, and offered it to the volunteers to drink.

By the end of that day most of the assembled Sikhs had shared the drink, and vowed their steadfast loyalty to their religion. And so was born the Khalsa, the brotherhood of Sikhs.
▶F&F.

Customs at Christmas

At Christmas, Christians remember the birth of Jesus Christ nearly 2000 years ago. It is also a joyous celebration to brighten up the dark days in the middle of winter, and many Christmas customs come from midwinter festivals which people held long before the Christians chose it as a time to have their own great celebration.

There is a calendar from CE 366 which shows that by this time Christians in Rome were already celebrating Christ's birthday on December 25th. But for a very long time that date had already been an important festival in Rome – The Birthday of the Unconquered Sun – when bonfires were lit to

December

show that the sun's light would steadily grow stronger over the coming months as winter gave way to spring.

There was another Roman festival which took place on December 17th – the Saturnalia, dedicated to the Roman god Saturn, worshipped as the god of growth. Everyone had a week's holiday, gave each other presents (particularly candles), feasted, and played games. Even slaves were freed for a day.

There was also a Jewish festival of light around this time, Hannukah, which is still celebrated nowadays.

Thus, many of the customs followed by the early Christians were Roman customs to which the Christians gave new meaning. The festival to the sun, the all-powerful source of light, was changed to a celebration of the light of Jesus Christ's entry into the world.

Presents were exchanged, just as in the festival of Saturnalia. But for the Christians they were in memory of the gifts from the wise men to the infant Jesus, after following the star and seeing the child in the stable in Bethlehem.

Customs from other parts of the world mingled with these. Throughout the northern half of the world, mid-winter had always been a time of celebration, to make sure that light would triumph over darkness, that spring would come and banish the deep cold of winter. Especially in Scandinavia, but also in many other countries, evergreen plants had been used to show life continuing through winter – particularly plants which had berries, for these fruits showed that there was further life to come. This is where we get the traditional decorations of holly and ivy, and the fir tree. The fir tree was first used in Germany about 1200 years ago, but it came to Britain much more recently – introduced by Queen Victoria's German-born husband, Prince Albert.

The lights of Christmas follow the customs of many festivals of light which have been held at this season for thousands of years. Of course they have their special meaning for Christians.

The yule log, a log cut from a tree which bears fruit, was a very important tradition. It burned for many days to celebrate the return of the sun following the shortest day of the year. Later, the yule log became a central part of Christmas celebrations. Even the traditional Christmas pudding, originally ball-shaped and carried to the table in flames, was once a symbol of the sun.

The crib – in memory of the manger in which Jesus lay – is one symbol which is entirely Christian. The traditional mince-pies are a very ancient custom in Britain, and were once made in the shape of the manger. They were filled with exotic foods and spices in memory of the wise men's gifts to the new-born Jesus.

Christmas cards are a lot more recent. They date from about 140 years ago.

Santa Claus is the result of a mixture of traditions and legends from different parts of the world. The original Santa Claus was a Bishop in Asia 1600 years ago. He was called St Nicholas, and was famous for his generous nature. Dutch sailors took the legends about him back to Holland, where Sinter Klaas, as he is called, is said to bring presents for children on December 6th, St Nicholas Day. He is always shown riding a white horse.

American children began to think of Santa Claus travelling from the North Pole, with a sledge and reindeer; we have followed this tradition in Britain. And instead of being associated with December 6th, he has become part of the celebration of Christmas, and is said to bring his gifts when all the gifts are exchanged, on Christmas Day, December 25th.

Note to readers

To refer you to relevant material, including songs, in other Ward Lock Educational books we have used this symbol ▶
See page 4

In Bethlehem town

Traditional French carol
translated by Roger Fiske

1 To Bethlehem town
Came Joseph and Mary, (repeat)
Begged shelter in vain.
Although they were weary –
'No room at the inn'.
Replies did not vary:
'No room at the inn,
No room at the inn.'

2 Good Joseph then gazed
On Mary his dearest; (repeat)
'What shall we do now,
What place would be nearest?'
He tenderly said,
'What place would be nearest
To grant us a bed?'
He tenderly said.

3 'Come, let us walk on,
Nor fear any danger; (repeat)
We'll find nothing here.'
And soon in a manger
She cradled her son;
And soon in a manger
She cradled her son,
God's holiest One.

4 Bring gifts to Him now;
Ye shepherds, adore Him; (repeat)
This baby's your King.
All bowing before Him
The angels shall sing;
All bowing before Him
The angels shall sing
To our new-born King.

▶FCYC

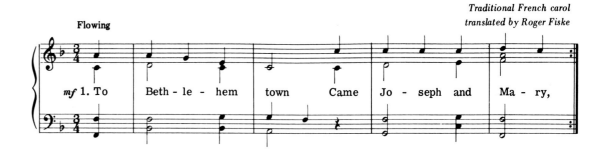

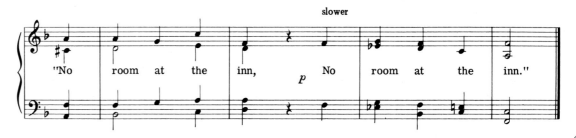

On a Christmas night

Words by Louise B. Scott
Music by Lucille F. Wood

On a lovely Christmas night
Shepherds travelled far,
Seeking Baby Jesus,
Following a star.
Shepherds came to Bethlehem,
Heard the angels sing,
Found a little manger
And the new-born King!

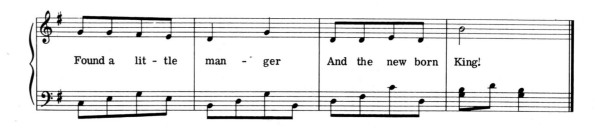

▶FCYC

46

Spring Term

January

In some years the following festivals may occur in January:

Guru Gobind Singh's Birthday. *See* December page 43.

Chinese New Year falls between January 21st and February 19th. *See* page 52. ▶ F&F and MCF.

January's name

This month gets its name from Janus, the ancient Roman god. He was god of gates and doorways, the protector of the beginnings of all things.

The ancient Romans believed he had two faces. With them, he could watch both sides of the gates into Roman cities. In the same moment he could see inside and outside homes, defend all doorways, protect the way in and the way out of every building.

There is a story that during one of the Romans' many wars, Janus defeated a plot to betray them to their enemies. Ever after, his temple was open in time of war, in case they should need his help again.

He reigned over the dawn of a new day. The Romans honoured him on the first day of every month, and at the beginning of a new year.

With one of his faces he looked back at the past year. With the other, he looked forward to the fresh starts and bright hopes of the year to come. So the first month of their calendar took Janus's name, and when the Roman calendar came into use in this country, we took that name for our first month too – January.

4 January

Louis Braille was born in 1809. *See* February 22nd.

6 January

Epiphany or Twelfth Night, the end of the Christmas season. Celebrates the visit of the Wise Men to Jesus. ▶ MCF.

10 January

This is what it was like to get a letter 150 years ago. You would hear a knock at your door. A man would be standing there, holding a large, folded sheet of paper. He would ask you to pay before handing it over. The cost would probably be very high, particularly if the letter had come a long way, or contained several sheets of paper.

You might not have the money to pay. And when you said so, away the man would go again, taking your letter with him.

Nowadays you would think it very rude if someone wrote to you without putting a stamp on the letter. But 150 years ago there were no such things as stamps. Very few letters were paid for by the sender. And the further the letter travelled, the more it cost. Here is how one postmaster described it at the time:

'The price of a letter is a great tax on poor people. I sent one, charged eightpence, to a poor labouring man about a week ago; it came from his daughter. He first refused taking it, saying it would take a loaf of bread from his other children; but, after hesitating a little time, he paid the money and opened the letter. I seldom return letters of this kind to Bristol, because I let the poor people have them, and take the chance of being paid; sometimes I lose the postage, but generally the poor people pay me by degrees.'

On January 10th 1840, something happened to change all this. It was something brilliantly simple, and totally new – the idea of a man named Rowland Hill. From this day on, all letters would be paid for by the sender. And they would cost the same (one penny) no matter how far they went.

Rowland Hill had two other startling new suggestions. Here's how he described one of them:

'Every house might be provided with a box into which the Letter-carrier would drop the letters, and, having knocked, he would pass on as fast as he could walk.'

Secondly, as a way of showing that postage had been paid, he suggested using a very small piece of paper, with some kind of gum on the back.

And so the letterbox and the postage stamp were born.

The first post office letter box in Fleet Street

The first stamps went on sale in May of 1840. They showed a portrait of Queen Victoria, and were called the Penny Black and the Twopenny Blue.

There were scenes of great excitement all over the country when the penny post began. Overnight it suddenly cost so little that most people could afford to send a letter, some of them for the first time in their lives. One eye-witness described the scene at the Head Post Office in London:

'The great hall was nearly filled with spectators, marshalled in a line by the police to watch the crowds pressing, scuffling, and fighting to get first to the window . . . Formerly one window sufficed to receive letters. On this evening six windows with two receivers at each were bombarded by applicants. As the last quarter of an hour approached, and the crowd still thickened, a seventh window was opened . . . and we learnt that on this evening upwards of 3000 letters had been posted at St Martin's Le Grand (the Head Post Office) between five and six . . . When the window closed, the mob, delighted at the energy displayed by the officers, gave one cheer for the Post Office, and another for Rowland Hill.'

Nowadays more letters are sent in a few days than were sent in a whole year before Rowland Hill's brilliant new ideas were first used. It's strange to think that stamps and letterboxes, things that we probably think nothing of, could once have caused such excitement and made such a difference in people's lives!

The story of fire

In winter, our thoughts turn to keeping warm, to fires, and how to shield ourselves against the cold.

Learning how to make and use fire was one of the most important discoveries early people made, and for thousands of years they have told stories about how this happened.

Here is one of them. It tells how the mighty Greek god Prometheus took earth and water, and in his enormous hands he kneaded it to a fine, smooth clay. Then, from it, he moulded figures, small, perfect, so beautiful they might have been children of the gods themselves. They were the first humans.

The goddess Athene breathed life into them, and Prometheus set them to live on earth. He taught them to know the forests and hills, to find food among wild berries and fruits, to seek water in pure streams, to find cool caves as shelter from the merciless sun.

But then, the first snows of winter fell from the grey skies, and icy winds pierced their flesh. Even their blood and bones began to freeze. Pitifully they huddled in their misery, knowing nothing of how to warm themselves, nothing of how to clothe and shield their bodies from that murderous blast.

Prometheus watched them, sorrowing. He saw their ignorance and fear. He saw, too, that they would die.

Unless he saved them. Only the gift of fire could help them now.

He knew too, that knowledge of fire was forbidden them. Zeus, Lord of Gods, god of the sky, lord of thunder and lightning, had forbidden it.

Yet Prometheus could not watch his people die in the first winter of their innocent lives. They must survive, must learn, must grow . . . They *must* have fire. He, Prometheus, must bring it to them.

Zeus' anger would be terrible. Even more terrible would be his punishment. But it was a price that Prometheus had to pay. Swiftly he moved through the black night, silently, stealthily, deep into the caverns of the earth, to the great black-smith's forge where the fire of the gods burned eternally. Here the thunderbolts of Zeus himself were forged, hammered in the white-hot streams of sacred fire.

Swiftly he seized a glowing coal, and wrapped it in a stalk of green fennel, to keep the flame alive. Then back across the unlit night he moved, towards the dying creatures of the earth . . .

And so people were given fire, and lived. Prometheus taught them to use it, how it could warm their bodies, cook their food, bake clay for pots and bowls. How it could melt metal for their tools and give them light through hours of gloom and darkness.

Thousands of years passed. In time, Zeus looked down at earth, curiously. Where once only the glow of moon and stars had lit the night, now pin-points of fire gleamed throughout the earth.

A roar of thunderous rage boomed across the world. Prometheus, below on earth, felt the jarring rush of wind and rain, felt the searing burn of lightning strike the earth, and knew that Zeus had seen his disobedience, and now would bring his terrible revenge.

For Prometheus, fire-bringer, a monstrous, lingering punishment, a torture that would last a thousand years.

But *that* is another story . . .

17 January

Robert Scott and his party reached the South Pole. *See* December 14th.

Old Twelfth Night. ▶MCF.

How calendars began

It is officially a new year in this country. In some other countries, and among people of various religions in this country, the new year will not begin until the spring or even the autumn.

The story of how we come to have a 12-month calendar begins as long as 6000 years ago. As soon as people began to sow, plant and harvest crops, they also needed to keep a record of the passing of time. They wanted to sow seed at the right season, in warmth, with enough rain to water the land. They needed the crops ready to harvest before the bad weather could harm them.

The first measure of time they used was the day – the time between one sunrise and the next. The next measure was the number of days between the appearance of one new moon and the next. This was called a month.

But farming people needed to know when the seasons would change, from winter to spring or from summer to autumn. And so they noted the number of months in each season, and how long it was from one spring to the next. This period they called a year. It was roughly 12 of the moon's months – or what we now call 'lunar' months.

Unfortunately, it was not exactly 12 lunar months. The whole year's seasons actually took 11 days longer. These extra days had to be added to the lunar calendar to make it work properly.

Just over 2000 years ago, the ancient Romans began the kind of calendar we use in this country now. They divided the year into 12 months, but no longer months based on the moon. Instead they were just 12, roughly equal, periods of time. They also began the year in January, instead of spring or autumn, as some countries did.

This is the kind of calendar used in countries where the main religion is Christian. There have been further changes since the time of the ancient Romans. Most countries also use it as the base of the calendar which controls their business and government life.

But people of the Hindu, Sikh, Buddhist, Muslim and Jewish religions use lunar calendars for their religious and festival year. Many celebrations take place at the new or full moon.

And people of different religions each choose an event in their own history from which to start numbering the years. The official number of the year in this country is counted from Jesus Christ's birth. So [1986] means that it is one thousand, nine hundred and eighty six years since the birth of Jesus. Interestingly, however, the date used for this is now believed to be wrong. Jesus was probably born 6 or 7 years earlier.

People of the Jewish religion number their years from when their tradition says the world was created, 3760 years before Christ's birth.

For Muslims, the important event was Mohammed's flight from Mecca to Medina, so they start counting from 622 years after the birth of Christ.

And in India there could be 136 years difference between the dates used by people in different parts of the country.

So the year that was called 1984 in this country was 1405 for Muslims, 5744 for Jews, and for Indians it was 1906 or 2042, depending on where they live.

See also July page 100.

The other side of the world

At this time of the year it is difficult to imagine what it is like to suffer from extreme heat and thirst. But in the southern half of the world – countries like Australia – this is the hottest time of the year. Parts of the country are desert – 'mile after shimmering mile of ridge and dune . . . heat-hazed, sun drenched, waterless.'

If you do not know how to find water you will die very quickly. People can live for several weeks without solid food, but can survive for only 10 days without fresh water.

This is part of a story about two children whose plane crashes in an Australian desert. They know nothing of how to stay alive, and can find neither food nor water. But a young aborigine boy finds them, collapsing in exhaustion . . .

'He spoke softly, urgently, the pitch of his words rising and falling like the murmur of wavelets on a sandy shore. The words themselves were meaningless; but his gestures spoke plainly enough. If they stayed where they were they would die: the bush boy fell to the sand, his fingers scrabbling the dry earth . . . But if they followed him he would take them to water; the bush boy swallowed and gulped. They hadn't far to go: only as far as the hill-that-had-fallen-out-of-the-moon; his finger pointed to a strange outcrop of rock that rose like a gargantuan cairn out of the desert, a cairn the base of which was circled by a dark, never-moving shadow.

It looked very far away.

The girl wiped the sweat out of her eyes. In the shade of the heartleaves it was mercifully cool; far cooler than it would be in the desert. It would be so much easier, she thought, to give the struggle up, simply to stay where they were. She looked at the cairn critically. How could the bush boy know there was water there? Whoever heard of finding water on top of a pile of rock in the middle of a desert?

'Arkooloola,' the bush boy insisted. He said it again and again, pointing to the base of the cairn.

The girl looked more closely, shading her eyes against the glare of the sun. She noticed that there was something strange about the shadow at the foot of the cairn. As far as she could see, it went all the way round. It couldn't, then, be ordinary shadow, caused by the sun. What else, she wondered, could create such a circle of shade? The answer came suddenly, in a flood of wonder and disbelief. It must be vegetation. Trees and bushes: thick, luxuriant, verdant, and lush. And such vegetation, she knew, could only spring from continually-watered roots. She struggled to her feet.

It seemed a long way to the hill-that-had-fallen-out-of-the-moon. By the time they got there the sun was setting.

They came to the humble-bushes first, the twitching, quivering leaves tumbling to the sand as they approached. Then came the straw-like mellowbane, and growing amongst them a grass of a very different kind: sturdy reed-thick grass, each blade tipped with a black, bean-shaped nodule: rustling death-rattle, astir in the sunset wind. The bush boy snapped off one of the reeds. He drove it into the sand. Its head, when he pulled it out, was damp. He smiled encouragement . . .

Peter had been lagging behind – for the last mile Mary had been half-carrying, half-dragging him. But now, like an iron filing drawn to a magnet, he broke loose and went scurrying ahead. He disappeared into the shade of the umbrella ferns, and a second later Mary heard his hoarse, excited shout.

'It's water, Mary! Water.'

'Arkooloola,' the bush boy grinned.

Together black boy and white girl pushed through the tangle of fern until they came to a tiny pear-shaped basin carved out of solid rock by the ceaseless drip of water. Beside the basin Peter was flat on his face, his head, almost up to his ears, dunked in the clear translucent pool. In a second Mary was flat out beside him. Both children drank, and drank, and drank.

The bush boy drank only a little. Soon he got to

his feet, climbed a short way up the cairn, and settled himself on a ledge of rock. Warm in the rays of the setting sun, he watched the strangers with growing curiosity. Not only, he decided, were they freakish in appearance and clumsy in movement, they were also amazingly helpless: untaught, utterly incapable of fending for themselves: perhaps the last survivors of some peculiarly backward tribe. Unless he looked after them, they would die. That was certain.'

Walkabout by James Vance Marshall

In this story the aborigine bush boy has knowledge which the white children do not have. They learn to value him and what he can teach them.

If he were plunged into their kind of life, in a different place, he would probably need their help just as much as they need his now.

Everyone has skills and knowledge which are of great value.

Darwin's discoveries

In December 1831, more than 150 years ago, a ship called *The Beagle* was sent by the British Navy to investigate the land, animals and plants of the South American coasts and islands in the Pacific. On board was a young man named Charles Darwin. He knew he was beginning a very exciting venture. He did not know that it would change his whole life. That journey would lead him to develop daring and very new ideas, ideas which would make him famous all over the world.

The voyage lasted nearly five years. It took Darwin westwards across the Atlantic, the Pacific and the Indian Oceans. He spent months in steaming jungles, explored barren volcanic islands, made expeditions across desert plains and into high rocky mountains. He kept a diary of everything he saw – birds and beetles, plants and animals, rocks

and their fascinating fossils (the skeletons of animals and plants embedded in rock). He began to realise that these fossils had come from animals and plants that existed a very long time ago.

Everything he saw made him think that all forms of life had developed slowly over millions of years, and were still developing and changing. The forms that survived did so because they were suited to the place they lived in – its temperature and climate, its land and foods.

Nowadays these ideas do not seem at all strange or new. But in Darwin's time they caused an uproar, for they challenged everything people

January

believed about how the world was formed. People were firmly convinced that all forms of life – animals, plants and humans – had always been the same, that they had never changed. Many were particularly angry about Darwin's suggestion that humans were descended from apes.

But there were many who began to think as he did, who thought that Darwin's ideas made a lot of sense.

Reading Darwin's diary of the voyage, it is easy to see what a keen and observant eye he had, and how carefully he made notes of the minutest details. In January 1832, soon after the voyage began, they reached the Cape Verde Islands in the Atlantic Ocean. Here is what he wrote:

'I was much interested, on several occasions, by watching the habits of an Octopus, or cuttle-fish. Although common in the pools of water left by the retiring tide, these animals were not easily caught. By means of their long arms and suckers, they could drag their bodies into very narrow crevices; and when thus fixed, it required great force to remove them. At other times they darted tail first, with the rapidity of an arrow, from one side of the pool to the other, at the same instant discolouring the water with a dark chestnut-brown ink. These animals also escape detection by a very extraordinary, chameleon-like power of changing their colour. They appear to vary their tints according to the nature of the ground over which they pass: when in deep water, their general shade was brownish purple, but when placed on the land, or in shallow water, this dark tint changed into one of a yellowish green. The colour, examined more carefully, was a French grey, with numerous minute spots of bright yellow: the former of these varied in intensity; the latter entirely disappeared and appeared again by turns. These changes were effected in such a manner, that clouds, varying in tint between a hyacinth red and a chestnut-brown, were continually passing over the body. Any part, being subjected to a slight shock . . . became almost black: a similar effect, but in a less degree, was produced by scratching the skin with a needle . . .

This cuttle-fish displayed its chameleon-like power both during the act of swimming and whilst remaining stationary at the bottom. I was much amused by the various arts to escape detection used by one individual, which seemed fully aware that I was watching it. Remaining for a time motionless, it would then stealthily advance an inch or two, like a cat after a mouse; sometimes changing its colour: it thus proceeded, till having gained a deeper part, it darted away, leaving a dusky train of ink to hide the hole into which it had crawled.

While looking for marine animals, with my head about two feet above the rocky shore, I was more than once saluted by a jet of water, accompanied by a slight grating noise. At first I could not think what it was, but afterwards I found out that it was this cuttle-fish, which though concealed in a hole, thus often led me to its discovery.'

The Voyage of the Beagle Charles Darwin

Chinese New Year

Now is the time of the Chinese New Year festival. Chinese people give each new year the name of an animal. This, for example, is the year of the . . . [1986 Tiger].

Here is one of the stories about how this custom began. It has been told for thousands of years.

The old year was nearly over. The animals waited eagerly for the new year to begin. This one was going to be particularly interesting, for the gods had decided to give it a name. And, even better, they were going to name it after one of the animals.

But which animal would it be? They all had their own ideas about that!

Dragon loomed high over the others, breathing flames and smoke as fiercely as he could.

'I am the most terrifying of you all,' he boomed. 'Give my name to the new year. Call it "the Year of the Dragon".' And he roared again, just to impress them a bit more.

Monkey skipped and swung from tree to tree. 'Look what I can do,' he screeched above their heads, 'Name the year after me. Name it "the Year of the Monkey".'

'Name it after me,' whinnied Horse, 'see how

elegant and fine and strong I am,' and he reared and snorted proudly before them.

'No, name it after me,' said Pig.

'After me,' hissed Snake

'After me . . .' 'After me . . .'

In turn Cockerel, Rat, Ox, Hare, Tiger, Ram and Dog all strutted and pranced and made their very best noises, so that the gods would be sure to notice and choose *their* name for the coming new year.

Instead, the gods grew so weary of the quarrelling that they decided to stop the argument once and for all.

'This is how we will decide,' they said. 'There will be a race across the great river. We will name

the coming year after whichever one of you wins.'

Now this seemed a good idea. The animals were extremely pleased with it, for each was certain that *he* was going to win.

And so, with much splashing and gurgling and blowing and snorting, the great race began.

Ox was strong. Easily he swam far ahead of all the others.

Rat was not so strong. But on the other hand, he was very, very cunning. As fast as he could, he paddled until he reached Ox's tail. He grasped it firmly and pulled himself up onto the broad, solid back.

Ox felt the tickle. 'It must be water lapping on my back.' he thought. And he swam on, thinking only of how he would be the winner of this very important race.

But as he reached the other bank of the river, Rat leapt right over his head and landed, *in front of him,* on dry land!

Ox stared. He was so shocked he could think of nothing to say.

The gods laughed. 'You were strong and fast, Ox,' they said. 'But Rat was clever, so he reached this side of the river first. We will give his name to the new year. It will be the Year of the Rat.'

'But as you were second, the next year will have your name, Ox – the Year of the Ox.'

And as each animal finished the race, the gods named a year after them. Tiger was third, so the third year got his name. Hare was fourth, Dragon fifth. Snake came next, followed by Horse, then Ram, Monkey, Cockerel, Dog. And last of all, Pig came grunting in, twelfth, looking as though he had swallowed all the water in the river.

So the first twelve years got their names. And after every twelve years, the list of names starts again, with the Year of the Rat, then the Year of the Ox, and then each of the others, in exactly the

same order as the animals finished that race so long ago, watched in amusement by the gods.

That is how this year came to be known as . . . [1986 Year of the Tiger].

Rat	1984	1996
Ox	1985	1997
Tiger	1986	1998
Hare	1987	1999
Dragon	1988	2000
Snake	1989	2001
Horse	1990	2002
Ram	1991	2003
Monkey	1992	2004
Cockerel	1993	2005
Dog	1994	2006
Pig	1995	2007

24 January

Now is a time of particular celebration in the snow-bound arctic regions of the world. It is the first sun-rise for more than two months. The sun sets in November, and does not rise again for 66 days.

Here is part of a story about an Eskimo girl named Miyax, whose American name is Julie. She runs away from home and lives on the frozen plains of Alaska among the wolves. Lying in the wolf den, she remembers times past, on the first dawn after the long Arctic night.

'January twenty-fourth was a day of celebration. Beginning about the twenty-first, the top of the world began to glow like an eclipse as the sun circled just below the horizon. The Americans began to smile and the Eskimos put away their winter games of yo-yo and darts. Excitement mounted higher and higher each day.

The morning of the twenty-fourth Julie and

January

Pearl ran all the way to school, for this was the most beautiful day of the year, the day of the sunrise.

Just after noon Julie and her classmates put on their parkas and mittens and skipped out the school door in awesome silence. The gussak principal was already outside watching the southeastern sky anxiously. His face seemed to say he really did not believe the miracle would happen.

'There it is!' a little boy shouted, as a brilliant light, first green then red, exploded on the horizon. Slowly the life-giving star arose until it was round and burning red in the sky. The Eskimos lifted their arms and turned their palms to the source of all life. Slowly, without any self-consciousness, every gussak raised his arms, too. Not one person snickered at the old Eskimo tradition.

For an hour and a half the sun moved above the horizon, reminding the Eskimos that the birds and mammals would come back, that the snow would melt, and that the great ice pack that pressed against the shore would begin to retreat and set them free to hunt and fish . . .

'Bright sun, I missed you so,' Julie whispered, and her palms felt vibrant with life.'

Julie and the Wolves Jean Craighead George

25 January

Today Burns Night is celebrated. It is a time when the people of Scotland honour their greatest poet, Robert Burns. He was born on January 25th nearly 230 years ago (1759) and wrote his first song when he was sixteen.

This is part of one of his poems. It is based on an old Scottish song from harvest celebrations, and when he wrote it, Burns was thinking of ancient stories about the spirit of the barleycorn. These stories tell how the spirit is driven out when the corn is threshed, to live in the barn through the winter. When the new crop is sown in the spring, the spirit returns to the fields, to give new life to the young corn shoots.

In the poem Burns is really telling the life-story of corn – how first it comes to life with the spring rains. How it grows and ripens through the summer months. How in the autumn the reapers come to cut it down and cart it away to be threshed and winnowed, left in water, and raked on the malt-house floor. Lastly it is dried in an oven and then mashed, ready for brewing.

John Barleycorn *A ballad*

There was three kings into the east,
Three kings both great and high,
And they hae sworn a solemn oath
John Barleycorn should die.

They took a plough and plough'd him down,
Put clods upon his head,
And they hae sworn a solemn oath
John Barleycorn was dead.

But the chearful Spring came kindly on,
And show'rs began to fall;
John Barleycorn got up again,
And sore surpris'd them all.

The sultry suns of Summer came,
And he grew thick and strong,
His head weel arm'd wi' pointed spears,
That no one should him wrong.

The sober Autumn enter'd mild
When he grew wan and pale;
His bending joints and drooping head
Show'd he began to fail.

His colour sicken'd more and more,
He faded into age;
And then his enemies began
To show their deadly rage.

They've taen a weapon, long and sharp,
And cut him by the knee;
Then ty'd him fast upon a cart,
Like a rogue for forgerie.

They laid him down upon his back,
And cudgell'd him full sore;
They hung him up before the storm,
And turn'd him o'er and o'er.

They filled up a darksome pit
With water to the brim,
They heaved in John Barleycorn,
There let him sink or swim.

They laid him out upon the floor,
To work him farther woe,

And still, as signs of life appear'd,
They toss'd him to and fro.

They wasted, o'er a scorching flame,
The marrow of his bones;
But a Miller us'd him worst of all,
For he crush'd him between two stones.

Robert Burns

26 January

Australia Day, commemorating the founding of the colony of New South Wales in 1788. ►MCF.

27 January

Nowadays television is very much a part of our lives. Most homes have a television set, and we use it both to entertain ourselves, and for teaching and studying.

It is difficult to imagine what life would be like without TV. It is not so long ago, however, that there was no such thing. Here is a report which appeared in *The Times* newspaper in 1926. It described a startling new event which took place on January 27th of that year: 'The Televisor – successful test of new apparatus.' It told how visitors to a laboratory in Soho, London, were shown the new apparatus by the inventor, John Logie Baird.

'First on a receiver in the same room as the transmitter and then on a portable receiver in another room, the visitors were shown recognisable reception of the movements of the dummy head and a person speaking. The image . . . was faint and often blurred, but substantiated a claim that through the 'Televisor' as Mr Baird has named his apparatus, it is possible to transmit and reproduce instantly the details of movement and such things as the play of expression on the face.

It has yet to be seen to what extent further developments will carry Mr Baird's system towards practical use.'

Only a short while before, Baird had demonstrated his new machine to the public at the London shop, Selfridges.

That clumsy television was made of wood and card, and the way it showed pictures of events taking place in another room alarmed some people, so much so that some newspapers asked whether this strange machine could see through brick walls and would invade people's private lives.

Baird had made his first working television only a year before. It was an extraordinary contraption, made from, among other things, a knitting needle, the lid of a hatbox, an electric fan motor, and lots of torch batteries, all put together on top of an old tea-chest. Yet, within four years, the BBC made its first television broadcast to the public. The announcer had to be rather an energetic person. He had to speak first into a microphone and then move swiftly into view of the camera.

At this time there were only thirty television sets in Britain, and the pictures were blurred, dim images which flickered a great deal.

But developments followed swiftly. There was such enormous excitement and interest in the new entertainment that many enthusiasts began to build their own television sets. Soon there was also the first television play. It was rather different from those we are used to seeing now, for only the actors' heads were shown – and only one at a time, dim and flickering as always.

Nowadays, when we have colour television with news, reports from very distant countries, plays, sports of every kind, and when we can receive pictures of events from the other side of the world almost as soon as they have happened, what a lot there is to show that *Times* reporter who wrote, only about 60 years ago, 'It has yet to be seen to what extent further developments will carry Mr Baird's system towards practical use'!

28 January

Today in Finland there is a festival called Kalevala Day, held in honour of the national poem of Finland, *The Kalevala*. It is based on popular songs handed down over many centuries, and tells of the gods and heroes of ancient Finland. Here is the story about the birth of the world.

Luonnotar was maiden of the sky. High in the misty heavens she lived, alone. And she was lonely. The wide emptiness was cold. She longed for company. And so she let herself fall from the heavens to the ocean below, and there she floated on the white-crested waves, searching, yearning, searching for a resting place.

For 700 years she drifted on, but no life passed her by. She found no rest. And Luonnotar despaired . . .

But then, one day, a sudden movement in the air, the beat of wings, a spray of water at her side . . . and on the waves there was a bird – an eagle, landing. Searching, like Luonnotar, for a quiet place. On Luonnotar's knee, rising like a pinnacle of rock, he built his nest, and put his eggs, and sat on them.

A sudden burn on Luonnotar's knee caused her to move it violently, in shock. Away the eggs rolled, and broke. But from them sprang the earth. Their rich yellow yolks became the fiery sun, their gleaming whites the delicate faces of the moon.

From the fragments of their shells the stars and clouds were born, and Luonnotar moulded hills and valleys, mountains, plains. And then she slept. For Luonnotar, maiden of the sky, daughter of Nature, had reached her resting place at last.

February

In some years the following festivals may fall in February:

Ash Wednesday, the start of Lent.

Chinese New Year. *See* January page 52.

Mahashivarati (Hindu festival of the god Siva).

Purim (Jewish festival). ▶F&F.

Shrove Tuesday or Pancake Tuesday falls between February 3rd and March 9th. *See* songs on pages 60 and 61. ▶MCF.

Holi (Hindu festival). *See* page 62. ▶F&F.

February's name

This month gets its name from the second month in the calendar used by the ancient Romans, which they brought to this country when they conquered it.

We are not really certain what the name means. There is one story that it comes from the name of the Roman god, Februus, god of the dead, for February was believed to be his month. Certainly it is a month which can be so cold and grey that you wonder whether winter will ever end.

There is another story that it is named after the religious festival which the Romans held in the middle of the month. This festival was called Februare – meaning 'to purify', possibly because it was a time when the Romans prepared themselves for the coming of spring. Although spring is still some weeks away, people often need to remind themselves that it *is* getting closer, that the days are getting longer, and soon warmer weather will arrive.

1 February

National Freedom Day in the USA. ▶MCF.

2 February

Candlemas or Feast of the Purification, the Christian commemoration of the child Jesus being brought to the Temple. ▶MCF.

The long winter

This is a true story about an American family snowed in by storms and blizzards lasting seven long months. Their town is completely cut off on the frozen, endless prairie. No trains can reach them to bring food or fuel for the stove. There is no meat left, no butter, only a little fat-meat dripping to spread on bread. And a very small amount of flour – enough for one more baking.

But, as they find, winter never lasts for ever . . .

'Winter had lasted so long that it seemed it would never end. It seemed that they would never really wake up.

In the morning Laura got out of bed into the cold. She dressed downstairs by the fire that Pa had kindled before he went to the stable. They ate their coarse brown bread. Then all day long she and Ma and Mary ground wheat and twisted hay as fast as they could (it was the only fuel they had to burn on the fire.) The fire must not go out; it was very cold. They ate some coarse brown bread. Then Laura crawled into the cold bed and shivered until she grew warm enough to sleep.

Next morning she got out of bed into the cold. She dressed in the chilly kitchen by the fire. She ate her coarse brown bread. She took her turns at grinding wheat and twisting hay. But she did not ever feel awake. She felt beaten by the cold and the storms. She knew she was dull and stupid but she could not wake up.

There were no more lessons. There was nothing in the world but cold and dark and work and coarse brown bread and winds blowing. The storm was always there, outside the walls, waiting sometimes, then pouncing, shaking the house, roaring, snarling and screaming in rage.

Out of bed in the morning to hurry down and dress by the fire. Then work all day to crawl into a cold bed at night and fall asleep as soon as she grew warm. The winter had lasted so long. It would never end.

Pa did not sing his trouble song in the mornings any more. On clear days he hauled hay. Sometimes a blizzard lasted only two days. There might be three days of clear cold, or even four days, before the blizzard struck again. 'We're outwearing it,' Pa said. 'It hasn't got much more time. March is nearly gone. We can last longer than it can.'

'The wheat is holding out,' Ma said. 'I am thankful for that.'

The end of March came. April began. Still the storm was there, waiting a little longer now perhaps but striking even more furiously. There was the bitter cold still, and the dark storm days, the wheat to be ground, the hay to be twisted. Laura seemed to have forgotten summer; she could not believe it would come again. April was going by . . .

'It can't beat us!' Pa said.

'Can't it Pa?' Laura asked stupidly.

'No,' said Pa. 'It's got to quit sometime and we don't. It can't lick us. We won't give up.'

Then Laura felt a warmth inside her. It was very small but it was strong. It was steady, like a tiny light in the dark, and it burned very low but no winds could make it flicker because it would not give up.

They ate the coarse brown bread and went through the dark and cold upstairs to bed. Shivering in the cold bed Laura and Mary silently said their prayers and slowly grew warm enough to sleep.

Sometime in the night Laura heard the wind. It was still blowing furiously but there were no voices, no howls or shrieks in it. And with it there was another sound, a tiny, uncertain liquid sound that she could not understand.

She listened as hard as she could. She uncovered her ear to listen and the cold did not bite her cheek. The dark was warmer. She put out her hand and felt only a coolness. The little sound that she heard was a trickling of waterdrops. The eaves were dripping. Then she knew.

She sprang up in bed and called aloud, 'Pa! Pa! The Chinook is blowing!'

'I hear it, Laura,' Pa answered from the other room. 'Spring has come. Go back to sleep.'

The Chinook was blowing. Spring had come. The blizzard had given up; it was driven back to the north. Blissfully Laura stretched out in bed; she put both arms on top of the quilts and they were not very cold. She listened to the blowing wind and dripping eaves and she knew that in the other room Pa was lying awake, too, listening and glad. The Chinook, the wind of spring, was blowing. Winter was ended.'

The Long Winter Laura Ingalls Wilder

6 February
Waitangi or New Zealand Day. ▶MCF.

8 February
Birthday of William Henry Fox Talbot, inventor of the modern form of photography. *See* August 19th.

10 February
120 years ago, thousands of ships left British ports every year and disappeared without trace, never to be seen again. They were so rotten and so heavily loaded, that they sank to the bottom of the sea, often only a short distance out of port, and in nothing more than a strong breeze. Thousands of seamen disappeared with them.

Anyone could tell that the ships were going to sink, just by looking at them in the harbour. Yet they still steamed out. If a seaman, knowing his ship was unsafe, tried to escape, he could be imprisoned for breaking his agreement to work on it.

But there was a shipowner named James Hall, who made up his mind to stop the tragic loss of ships and men. In February 1870, he spoke to a meeting of businessmen in London, trying to persuade them that new laws should be passed. Shipowners (like himself) he was arguing, should be prevented from sending ships to sea in such a dangerous state.

These are his own words, describing how ships were 'so deeply laden as to have their main decks under water, and foundering after leaving port' and how 'passenger-carrying ships may in this month of February be seen leaving our ports with the arch-board on the stern of the ships, upon which the ship's name and port are generally painted, on a line with the water's edge.' 'The wonder,' he added, 'is not that so many ships are lost, but that the number is so few . . .'

That speech was a turning point, for one of the people listening to James Hall was a new member of Parliament, Samuel Plimsoll. He was appalled by what he heard, and decided to make sure that such horrors were stopped.

He was particularly interested in one of James Hall's suggestions – that a line be painted on the side of ships to show how much they should be loaded. As long as this line was *above*, or at least *level*, with the surface of the water, a ship was safe to put to sea. But if the ship dropped low enough for the line to be *below* the surface of the water, then the ship would be judged unsafe, and would not be allowed to leave the port.

The moment he left that meeting, Samuel Plimsoll set to work. First he visited James Hall, and found out more about his ideas. Then he collected all the information he could – how many ships were sunk, how many seamen drowned, what kind of state the ships were in, how much they were overloaded. He took photographs of the families of lost seamen, and of ships in every port. He wrote a famous book called *Our Seamen*. People were outraged by its stories of the deaths of people on British ships.

Plimsoll also travelled the country, making speeches to convince more and more people that new laws must be passed. Within four years he had succeeded. From then onwards, every ship had to have a line on its side, just as James Hall had suggested. And they still have them nowadays.

The line is called a Plimsoll line, after that energetic and dedicated Member of Parliament who worked so hard to make it happen.

Countries all over the world now use this method to make sure that a ship is not carrying too much weight. Over the years since the Plimsoll Line was first used, the lives of countless seamen and passengers have been saved.

The stag and the lion
A stag was drinking from a pool and saw himself mirrored in the surface of the water. 'How fine my antlers look!' he thought. 'But how weak and thin my legs are!'

As he stood there, thinking about this, a lion crept close and sprang at him. Away the stag leapt, and sped across the open plains, drawing further and further from the lion, until at last he ran into a wood. There his antlers caught, hard and fast in the spreading branches of the trees.

February

As the lion drew near, the stag cried out in despair, 'How foolish I have been. I thought nothing of my legs, which are strong and swift enough to save my life. And yet I took such pride in my antlers, and now they will be the death of me!'

What is worth most to us, we often value least.

Adapted from Aesop

12 February
Darwin was born in 1809. *See* January page 51.

14 February
Saint Valentine's Day. ▶MCF.

15 February
George Washington's birthday, a holiday in the USA in honour of the first American president. ▶MCF.

The search in the snow
February can be very cold, with heavy falls of snow and unexpected blizzards. For farmers caring for their animals, such weather can bring particular dangers. Here is a story about a farmer's struggle to help his sheep.

'I saw at once that not a moment must be lost, to save our stock. All the earth was flat with snow, all the air was thick with snow; more than this no man could see, for all the world was snowing . . .

With spades, and shovels, and pitchforks, and a round of roping, we four set forth to dig out the sheep; and the poor things knew that it was high time . . .

Watch, like a good and faithful dog, followed us very cheerfully, leaping out of the depth, which took him over his back and ears already, even in the level places; while in the drifts he might have sunk to any distance out of sight, and never found his way up again. However, we helped him now and then, especially through the gaps and gateways; and so after a deal of floundering, some laughter and a little swearing, we came all safe to the lower meadows, where most of our flock was hurdled.

But behold, there was no flock at all! None, I mean, to be seen anywhere; only at one corner of the field, the eastern end, where the snow drove in, in a great white billow, as high as a barn and as broad as a house. This great drift was rolling and curling beneath the violent blast . . . and all the while from the smothering sky, more and more fiercely at every blast, came the pelting pitiless arrows, winged with murky white, and pointed with the barbs of frost . . .

Watch began to scratch at once, and to howl along the side of it; he knew that his charge was buried there . . . But we four men set to in earnest, digging with all our might and main, shovelling away at the great white pile, and fetching it into the meadow. Each man made for himself a cave, scooping at the soft cold flux, which slid upon him at every stroke . . .

I laid my head well into the chamber; and there I heard a faint 'ma-a-ah', coming through some ells of snow, like a plaintive buried hope, or a last appeal. I shouted aloud to cheer him up, for I knew what sheep it was . . . And then we all fell to again; and very soon we hauled him out. Watch took charge of him at once, with an air of the noblest patronage, lying on his frozen fleece, and licking all his face and feet, to restore his warmth to him . . .

Then of the outer sheep (all now snowed and frizzled like a lawyer's wig) I took the two finest and heaviest and with one beneath my right arm, and the other beneath my left, I went straight home to the upper sheppey, and set them inside, and fastened them. Sixty-and-six I took home in that way, two at a time on each journey; and the work grew harder and harder each time, as the drifts of snow were deepening. No other man should meddle with them; I was resolved to try my strength against the strength of the elements; and try it I did, ay and proved it. A certain fierce delight burned in me, as the struggle grew harder; but rather would I die than yield; and at last I finished it. People talk of it to this day: but none can tell what the labour was, who have not felt that snow and wind.

Of the sheep upon the mountain, and the sheep upon the western farm, and the cattle on the upper burrows, scarcely one in ten was saved; do what we would for them. And this was not through any neglect (now that our wits were sharpened), but from the pure impossibility of finding them at all. That great snow never ceased a moment for three days and nights; and then when all the earth was filled, and the topmost hedges were unseen, and the trees broke down with the weight . . . a brilliant sun broke forth and showed the loss . . .

Lorna Doone R D Blackmore

An African story of fire

Here is a traditional story about how people came to have fire. All over the world, stories like this have been told for thousands of years. (You may remember the Greek story of Prometheus last month.)

However, different the lands, the climates and the customs of the people who have told them, these stories are often surprisingly similar. This one comes from West Africa.

The Creator made all things. He made the sea and earth. He made its mountains and valleys, its lakes and rivers. He made its animals and birds, its plants and trees, and the fish that swim in the sea.

And then he made people. He gave them knowledge, to build their shelters and find their food.

But he did not give them fire. This he kept far away, high in the heavens above the earth.

The people knew the Creator had fire. They knew it warmed his house when the night was cold and cooked his food, and gleamed in the darkness after the sun had fallen far below the hills.

So they said to the young boy, 'Go, visit the Creator. Ask him to share the warmth and power of fire with us.'

But the boy was wise. He knew his journey into heaven would be in vain, for never would the Creator willingly give fire away.

In his mind an idea was born. It took shape, and grew, and became a plan – a brave and daring plan of how he would find fire and bring it back to earth, and the Creator would not know it had been done until it was too late. Once given, the flame could not be taken away again.

In the cool of the evening, as the sun sank low over the trees, he left his home and travelled through the lengthening shadows across the earth and up into the heavens.

He arrived at the Creator's house just as the evening meal was being prepared.

'I have come to help,' he said. And, seeing that the boy was sturdy and strong, and willing to work hard, he was not turned away, but given tasks to do about the house, fetching and carrying as the food was cooked.

In wonder, he watched the bubbling cooking pots, the fierce, crackling flames. Never had he seen such glory.

Night fell, and the rooms grew dark. 'Go to the house of the Creator's wives,' he was told. 'Fetch a lighted lamp and bring it here.'

Now it was in the wives' house that the fire was kept, and so the boy was pleased to go. Now he could see how they lit the lamp from the flame which burned there all the time.

Carefully he carried the lamp back, marvelling at the heat that nearly burned his hands, at the light it threw so brightly into the night's blackness.

Days passed. He was no longer a stranger in the house. Again and again he went to fetch the lamps, and watched them lit in the flame of the Creator's hearth. Until the time when he was told to take the flame himself, and he was left alone there, at the hearth, with the fire.

Swiftly he took a brand, a flaming stick, and wrapped it in green plantain leaves to keep the flame alight. Then, tying a cloth around it, he seized some firewood and left the Creator's house, carrying his precious burden back to earth.

In time the Creator looked down from heaven. In every corner of the earth, smoke rose, whisping cheerfully from cooking fires, bright lamps gleamed . . .

In rage, he called his son. 'Find who has dared to steal fire from the hearth of the Creator's house,' he boomed.

The Creator's son went to the boy who had taken fire and asked, 'Is it you who has done this?'

The boy was afraid. He knew the Creator would now punish him. But he was truthful, and he gathered all his courage, saying, 'The people needed fire. I took it for them, and I brought it here.'

So angry was the Creator at this news, and seeing the boy standing there so bravely, daring to defy him, that he hurled a punishment to strike the boy at once.

From that time onwards, the boy always bore the mark of the Creator's wrath. No longer could he stand, tall and straight and strong. He limped. That was his punishment. And that is how he came to be called The Lame Boy who Brought Fire to Earth.

See also January page 49.

Pancake Tuesday

Pancake Tuesday,
It's Pancake Tuesday,
It's Pancake Day to-day.

1   So find the recipe,
    Can you guess if we
    Need two eggs or three?
    You can weigh the flour,
    I hope the milk's not sour,
    Then a pinch of salt is all we want,
    Butter and oil to fry them in.

    Pancake Tuesday, etc.

2   Why do we cook them?
    Have a look then
    Find out how it started:
    Lent was very near
    The larder must be clear —
    So put the batter in the pan
    This is how it all began.

▶ MCF pages 24, 25
▶ BBB No 35

60

French folk song
Words and arrangement
by Barrie Carson Turner

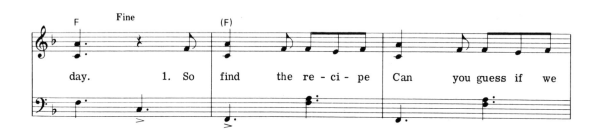

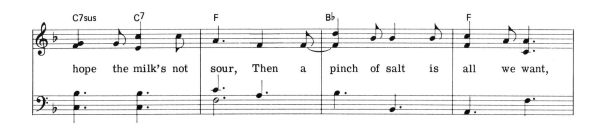

hope the milk's not sour, Then a pinch of salt is all we want,

1 **2** D.S. al Fine

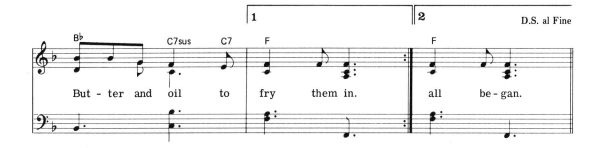

But - ter and oil to fry them in.   all be - gan.

Words by Christina Rossetti
Music by Frank Daunton

Mix a pancake

Brightly

Mix a pan-cake, stir a pan-cake, Pop it in the pan.

Fry the pan-cake, toss the pan-cake, Catch it if you can.

Mix a pancake, stir a pancake,
Pop it in the pan.
Fry the pancake, toss the pancake,
Catch it if you can.

February

20 February

On this day in 1896 the cinema came to Britain, when a programme of films was shown for the first time to a paying audience. *See* March 22nd.

22 February

Over 170 years ago in France, a small boy named Louis Braille skipped across a village road to play in his father's workshop. His father, the village saddler, was out. But in the workshop were great wooden workbenches, sharp tools all shapes and sizes, pieces of soft, shining leather, half-made saddles, rich smells of wood and soap and oils, and Louis was fascinated by these things.

Eagerly he clambered onto a chair. He searched the bench, and quickly found what he was looking for – a long, sharp tool. Now he could work just like his father! A beautiful round hole in a piece of leather – that's what he'd make.

Minutes later, there was a sudden scream of pain and terror. People ran towards the workshop. And there they found Louis, blood pouring down his face. As he bent over the leather, the tool had slipped and pierced his right eye.

He would never see again from that eye. Within two years the sight had gone from the other eye as well.

Yet not many years later, Louis Braille was going to give blind people the greatest gift they could have.

Imagine what it was like to be blind 170 years ago. It was usually impossible to do work of any kind. You could not read or write, so you could not study and learn as other people could. You would depend on other people for everything you needed.

Many had to beg in the streets – for this was the only way to get money and food. And because blind people were so often helpless and uneducated, they were usually treated differently from everyone else, as though they were not just blind, but also very stupid.

A very few learned to read books which were written in huge letters raised above the page, tracing the letter-shapes with their fingers. But it was very slow, and the books were large and heavy, for the letters were so big.

Louis was one of the few blind people who learned to read like this, for he went to a special school in Paris. When he was 12 years old, something very important happened. An army captain visited the school, to show them a new way of writing. He used it for sending messages between soldiers at night, and the letters were not at all like the usual letters of the alphabet. They were made with groups of dots, raised above the surface of the page.

The idea fascinated young Louis. The captain's system was too difficult – it needed so many dots to make each letter. No one could possibly remember them all, and writing a word would take a very long time. But he was certain it was possible to do it much more simply.

And so he set to work. He was now 13 years old. In every moment of spare time at school, he thought about it. During the holidays, it occupied hour after hour. He experimented with different groups of dots. He combined them in different ways. He used fewer and fewer, and still fewer.

At last he was satisfied. He had something simple and clear enough to be used swiftly and easily. It had taken him two whole years to work it out.

He was just 15 years of age. He had developed something that would open the door into a whole new world for people who could not see. Now, like anyone else, they could read and write. They could study and learn a trade or profession, prepare to earn a living for themselves. They could start to play a full part in the life of their villages and towns.

Louis' system was given his surname and called 'Braille'. On this day in 1844, it started to be taught in the school for the blind in Paris where Louis was once a pupil and later a teacher. It has now spread all over the world. Blind people in every country are reading and writing using it.

What an achievement for a young boy, so determined that others like him should live a full and useful life, learning all about the world they could not see and sharing its pleasures as much as anyone else!

The story of Prahlad

The Hindu festival of Holi is being celebrated now. There are several ancient stories which are told at this time. This is one of them.

There was once a king called Hiranyakashup. He was great and powerful, but he was also evil. One wish he had – that his power would grow and grow and grow, until he was lord of all the universe, a mighty god, mightier than any other, worshipped far and wide across the land.

He sent messengers to every corner of his kingdom. 'From now on,' they said, 'no worship of any god but Hiranyakashup is allowed. He is the only god, the all-powerful. Worship another on pain of death.'

In fear everyone obeyed. Everyone, that is, except one small boy. Prahlad, son of the king, would not. He was small, and he was very young. But he knew his father was not God. He saw the evil in him, the mad desire to rule the world unchallenged. And so he would not obey him, would not worship him.

Anger burned in the evil father, like a festering wound. He longed to punish the boy, to take revenge for his defiance. He was afraid, too, that others would hear of it, and perhaps rebel as well.

He must kill him. Again and again Hiranyakashup tried. Each time the boy survived. Each time the king's hatred became stronger, more vicious still.

He had a sister Holika, as evil as he. 'Let me take Prahlad,' she said. '*My* magic will kill him finally. No flame can burn me. No fire will be too powerful. But for the boy it will be certain death.'

And so saying, she seized Prahlad and leapt into a deadly fire. Upwards it flamed, burned stronger, soared above her head . . . and in that moment, as the flames engulfed her, Holika knew her magic could not work while she had Prahlad in the fire.

As Holika's shriek of mingled rage and terror was lost in the spurt and crackle of the fire, a figure appeared in its midst. A small, lone figure. Prahlad. Not a single hair was scorched, no burn had seared his skin. His steadfast belief in truth had protected him against all evil.

In time, the young Prahlad became the great King Prahlad, ruling as justly and wisely as his father had ruled with wickedness and greed.

During the festival of Holi, bonfires are lit in memory of the burning of evil Holika, of how she was defeated by the courage of a little boy who would not turn away from the truth.

In this celebration of the victory of good over evil, people are also rejoicing each year in the victory of warmth and the brightness of spring over the cold, dark gloom of winter.

Naming the days

Monday, Tuesday, Wednesday. Thursday, Friday, Saturday and Sunday. All these are named after ancient gods and goddesses worshipped by the Anglo-Saxons when the Romans conquered Britain.

But like many things in our calendar, we owe the names originally to the Romans themselves, for they are based on the days of the Roman week.

The Romans believed that the planets which they saw circling above the earth were gods. The Sun, Moon, Mars, Mercury, Jupiter, Venus and Saturn, all these were worshipped. They believed that they ruled over every hour of every day, and so each day was called after a god.

When the Roman calendar was brought to this country, these day-names were changed to those of the gods and goddesses already worshipped by the Anglo-Saxons.

Mars, Roman god of war, was replaced by Tiw, Anglo-Saxon god of war, and so Mars' day became

Woden, god of storm rain and harvest

Thor, the god of thunder

Tiw's day – from which we get our word Tuesday. It was once thought that a boy born on a Tuesday would be a great warrior.

The Roman Mercury was like the Saxon god Woden, so that day became Woden's day – or Wednesday.

Jupiter, god of thunder, was changed to the Saxon god of thunder, Thor. That's why we have a day named Thursday, from Thor's day.

Venus, Roman goddess of love, gave way to the Saxon love goddess, Frigg. Her day became Frigg's day or Friday, as it is now. It was always thought to be a lucky day to get married.

Together with Saturn's day (Saturday), Sun's day (Sunday) and Moon's day (Monday) this gives us all the days of our week.

February

29 February

This year is a leap year, and today is February 29th, a date which happens only once in four years.

We call it a leap year because people say that it 'leaps' over one of the days in the week. This is what they mean. In an ordinary year, there are 52 weeks and one extra day. So each year, January 1st will be *one day later* in the week than it was the year before. If January 1st is a Monday one year, it will be Tuesday the next year and Wednesday the year after.

But in a leap year there are 52 weeks and *two* extra days. The second extra day is added after February 28th and becomes February 29th, like today.

From now on, all the dates in the rest of the year

will be *two* days later in the week than they were last year. If March 1, (tomorrow), was a Sunday last year, it will not be Monday this year, but Tuesday. That is, it has 'leapt' right over Monday and landed on Tuesday – and hence the name 'leap year'.

And why does it leap? That is because most years our calendar gives us a year of 365 days,

whereas the year is really 365 and a quarter days long. So every fourth year, (the leap year) the four missing quarter-days are added together to make up one extra day, February 29th.
See also July page 100.

How people began

This is a story about how the first people were made. It comes from Guatemala in Central America.

In the beginning, when time began, there was nothing but water over the whole world – no land, no living things, only the empty waves, the storm winds of the air, and the mighty gods Hurukan and Gucamatz who soared above the grey waters; Hurukan, god of whirlwinds and the thunder, and his helper, Gucumatz, god of the living things to be, the plumed serpent.

And they said, 'Earth,' and out of the waters dry land rose. Mountains and hills burst from its smooth plains, valleys carved deep in its crust. Gucumatz moved across the earth, and wherever he passed, plants sprang from its soil, and trees, pure water flowed in rivers to moisten it.

But Hurukan and Gucumatz wanted other life on their new earth – living beings who would think and talk, and know who had made them, and kneel in thanks to their creators.

First they made animals, and set them free in the forests. But the animals could not speak, they did not understand that Hurukan and Gucumatz had given them life. They could not worship them.

Next they took clay, and moulded human figures from it. These were worse than the animals. They could not move or speak. Hurukan and Gucumatz destroyed them. Then they took living wood, and carved figures. These creatures moved, but still they could not understand enough to wor-

ship their creators. So they began to destroy them too.

However, they escaped, and lived in the forests among the trees. That is how monkeys came to be on earth.

At last Hurukan and Gucumatz took maize, plaiting and twisting yellow and white strands of the plant into the shapes of men.

At last, these men were perfect. They were wise, could speak, could move, had feelings, understanding . . .

Now Hurukan and Gucumatz were certain that they would be honoured and thanked for giving life.

But the men were far too perfect. Their eyesight was so strong that they could see right into the heavens where their creators lived. Hurukan and Gucumatz were not mysterious, awesome figures, striking wonder into men's hearts. And so they would not worship them.

One night, while the people slept, Hurukan and Gucumatz stole down amongst them and swiftly made their eyesight shorter. When they awoke, they could not see so far. The gods in heaven were now dim, almost unseen, shrouded in mists. They kneeled to honour them, and worship began.

In time Hurukan and Gucumatz made women to live among the men. They gave them fire that they might learn to tame the earth and use its riches . . .

So the first people began their life.

Note to readers

To refer you to relevant material, including songs, in other Ward Lock Educational books we have used this symbol ▶
See page 4

In some years the following festivals may fall in March:

Easter falls between March 22nd and April 24th. *See* page 70 and song on page 77. ▶MCF and F&F.

Holi (Hindu festival). *See* page 62. ▶F&F.

Shrove Tuesday falls between February 3rd and March 9th. *See* songs on pages 60 and 61. ▶MCF.

Mothering Sunday falls between March 4th and April 7th. *See* Class Assembly page 121. ▶MCF.

Passover (Jewish festival) falls between March 27th and April 24th. *See* page 71. ▶F&F and MCF.

March's name

March gets its name from Mars, one of the gods of ancient Rome. He is usually described as the god of war, but in very early times he was god of the spirit of new life in the earth, of the growth of plants and animals.

He roamed the forests and mountains, and people dedicated many animals and plants to him – the woodpecker, horse and wolf, the fig tree, oak and laurel.

He was also said to be the father of Romulus and Remus, the twin brothers who founded the city of Rome.

In time, however, Mars changed. He became the god of war, and other, less important gods began to watch over the brightness of spring instead of him. But the main festivals in honour of Mars were still celebrated at the beginning of spring, and this may be why the Romans gave his name to the third month in their calendar.

When we began to use their calendar, we too used the name of Mars for our third month, March.

1 March

Today is St David's Day in Wales, the feast day of their patron saint. It is a time when the Welsh people show their pride in being Welsh.

We actually know very little about St David (Dewi in Welsh). His story was first written down nearly 400 years after he died. Even the date of his death is not really known, although we think he died on March 1st in the year CE 589. His legend tells how he was born some 69 years earlier during a raging storm. He was the son of a Welsh chieftain, and grew up to become a monk. During his lifetime he founded many monasteries which became centres of great learning. His last great monastery was in the far corner of south-west Wales, in what is now known as St David's.

Long after he died, he was chosen as the patron saint of Wales, and on his day Welsh people display their national emblems, the daffodil and the leek.

We do not really know why the leek is used. St David's own emblem is the dove, the bird of peace. But there is one story of how David told Welsh soldiers to wear the leek during battle so that they could recognise each other easily.

St David's Day is at the beginning of spring, when daffodils are in bloom. So this beautiful flower has also become a Welsh national emblem. ▶MCF.

3 March

In 1899 Marconi's wireless was first used for the saving of life when a stranded ship, the *Elbe*, used it to call for help, and all the crew were saved. *See* December 12th.

National Day in Morocco. ▶MCF.

Alexander Graham Bell, inventor of the telephone born in 1847. *See* October 26th.

The terrors of avalanches

This is the time of year when people who live in mountain districts like the Swiss Alps may face the terrors of avalanches – those masses of snow and ice which hurtle down a mountain-side and sweep everything with them.

What is it like to live in a region where such things may happen? Here is part of a story about people whose village has been destroyed in such an avalanche. As rescue works begins, and there is a threat of more avalanches, they are sent to a safer place. Travelling through the snow-bound mountains, suddenly, inside a tunnel, their train screeches to a halt . . .

'A minute later a grey-haired ticket collector came in . . . He pushed his way through the crowded central gangway, nodding to right and left in a friendly way as he passed. He made reassuring gestures with both hands and it was only when the buzz of talk had died down that he began to speak.

'We've got stuck in a small avalanche. Nothing serious has happened. But if any of the passengers would care to help clear away the snow – we've a railway engineer with us on the train and he can use all the help he can get.'

A quarter of an hour later a couple of dozen passengers, mostly men and boys, were crowded round the front of the engine. The little train had

March

set out prepared for whatever might happen, and had brought enough tools to set a whole gang of helpers to work. The railway engineer who was travelling with them issued his instructions. Spades, picks and snow shovels did good service and many people worked with their hands to clear away the stones, torn off branches and masses of broken twigs that the snow had brought down with it. It was a landslide and had swept away everything that lay in its way for the whole length of its course, which ran down the mountain side in a fantastic cone of rubble. Only part of it had landed on the railway line, just in front of the mouth of the tunnel, and it was very lucky for everybody that the engine driver had jammed on his brakes at once.

The snow that had come down was black rather than white and smelled strongly of resin because of the freshly split pine wood. Very little was said. Even Paolo, who was working next to Werner, whispered when he had anything to say. White, feathery snow-flakes fell out of the grey sky and after an hour everything was pure white again: the slope down which the avalanche had rushed, the avalanche itself, the roof of the train and the shoulders of the men and boys working away in silence.

Once someone looked anxiously up the slope that the avalanche had come hurtling down. Could anyone be sure that the same thing would not happen again? How long had they been working? It seemed like hours. Would they ever get to Brachen? The snow scoops on the engine could do nothing against this tightly packed snow. Every spadeful of it weighed pounds and pounds.

The railway engineer had got in touch with Brachen station by wireless. The electric snow-plough was on the way, and twenty men belonging to the railway were working away at the other side of the avalanche. The line might be cleared that afternoon.

At about twelve the snow stopped. A quarter of an hour later the sun broke through. The passengers, digging sturdily away, were much more cheerful. Werner, who was sweating like a horse, laughed at Paolo's jokes and at Jean Pierre tumbling about in the snow . . .

Then, before anyone expected it, the engine whistled again. They're through! We can go on! cried Paolo.

But the young railway engineer standing on the step of the engine had other news for them. His face was drawn with anxiety as he shouted hoarsely: Into the train with you all at once! The engine's backing into the tunnel!

Everyone leapt for the train. There was no time to ask why. But the terror of the avalanche was clearly written on all their faces. Everything happened very quickly. The railway workers sprang on to the train as well and were carried into the tunnel. The little platforms at each end of the coaches were crammed full, the doors were not even closed.

There was a sudden thunderous roar followed by a deafening crash and the tinkle of falling glass. Everyone crouched down and clapped their hands over their ears. The blast blew through the tunnel like a hurricane. Paolo, with his mouth open, was flung over beside Werner, who pulled him up.

It was all over in a few seconds. One could feel a deep sigh of thankfulness go up from everyone. Thank God we were safely in the tunnel when it happened.

After a moment's deep hush an indescribable hubbub broke out, made up of every kind of human sound from crying and sobbing to hysterical laughter and happy shouts.'

Avalanche A Rutgers van der Loeff

This is a story of a great tragedy, for enormous damage is caused by the avalanches, and many people are killed. But it also a story of great courage.

The young people in particular show their bravery, for they are determined to find those who have been buried by the snow, despite their fear, their exhaustion and the bitter cold. Lives are saved and people reunited with those they thought they had lost. And everyone plays a part in this.

6 March
Independence Day in Ghana. ▶ MCF.

7 March
Birthday of Niépce, who took the world's first successful photograph in the 1820s. *See* August 19th.

10 March
The first sentence was spoken over the telephone in Alexander Graham Bell's laboratory in 1876. He said to his assistant 'Mr Watson, come here, I want you.' *See* October 26th.

11 March
Alexander Fleming, who discovered penicillin, died in 1955. *See* August 15th.

12 March
The birth in 1847 of the first baby whose mother had been given chloroform. *See* November 15th.

Second Monday in March

Today schools on every continent in the world are celebrating that they belong to the Commonwealth Community, and that this links them with nearly 1000 million other people, a quarter of the world's population.

At the moment there are 49 countries in the Commonwealth. Some have been members since the 1930s, others joined more recently, some only in the last few years. It includes nearly a quarter of the world's nations, – countries on every continent.

These are the members: Antigua and Barbuda, Australia, The Bahamas, Bangladesh, Barbados, Belize, Botswana, Britain, Brunei, Canada, Cyprus, Dominica, Fiji, The Gambia, Ghana, Grenada, Guyana, India, Jamaica, Kenya, Kiribati, Lesotho, Malawi, Malaysia, Maldives, Malta, Mauritius, Nauru, New Zealand, Nigeria, Papua New Guinea, St Christopher and Nevis, St Lucia, St Vincent and the Grenadines, Seychelles, Sierra Leone, Singapore, Solomon Islands, Sri Lanka, Swaziland, Tanzania, Tonga, Trinidad and Tobago, Tuvalu, Uganda, Vanuatu, Western Samoa, Zambia, Zimbabwe.

Some of these countries are large, like India, with 600 million people. Others, such as Tuvalu and Nauru in the Pacific Ocean, are much smaller, with 8000 people.

Some of the poorest countries in the world belong, as well as some of the wealthiest.

Today, together with schools throughout the Commonwealth, we are celebrating the richness of tradition and the different ways of life in all the Commonwealth countries. And we remember that our countries have joined together in order to work for peace in the world, for equality and a decent standard of living for all its people.

17 March
St Patrick's Day, the Irish celebration of their patron saint. *See* Class Assembly on page 120. ▶MCF.

The birth of spring

At this time of year, many stories are told about the birth of spring and the death of winter. Here is a very ancient tale from Japan. It tells of the quarrel between the light and warmth of the sun, and the wind and rain of storms. It tells of the coming of winter, the dark cold covering the earth. But in the end, the light and warmth of the sun returns, and with it, spring.

Ama-terasu, goddess of the sun, was so powerful that her brother Susa-no-wo, god of storms, grew jealous. He longed to rule heaven, just as she did, and he was angry that he could not.

He wept with rage, and the rain fell, turning the rivers and streams into torrents. He stamped his foot, and the earth shook. He roared, and thunder and lightning flashed, destroying the rice fields which Amu-terasu had sown in heaven.

Yet still his sister's worshippers prepared for harvest festivals. Enviously, Susa-no-wo threw filth into her temples. Shrieking with rage, he tore the roof off her palace and hurled a dead horse into the rooms below.

Now Amu-terasu was angry. She left the world and went into a deep, rocky cave in heaven. As she stepped inside, the earth plunged into cold and bitter darkness. All things withered, and evil spirits ruled the icy mists that covered everything.

The other gods were worried. The world was

March

dying without Ama-terasu's light, but she would not come out. Again and again they tried to tempt her. Nothing worked.

At last they had an idea. They hung a mirror outside the cave, bedecked with jewels and gaily coloured streamers. And then they held a festival, singing and dancing, cheering and laughing.

Ama-terasu heard the sound of celebration. She peeped out. She was so curious at her own reflection in the mirror, that she came a little further. At once the god of force seized her and dragged her out.

Now the sun beamed across the earth, and all the world was warm again. Evil spirits fled, and winter ended.

Susa-no-wo, god of storms was driven out of heaven, never to return.

Haiku for spring

Winter withering:
Sparrows strut
In the guttering.
Tan Taigi

Snow melting!
Deep in the hill-mist
A crow cawing.
Katō Gyōdai

The snow thaws —
And suddenly the whole village
Is full of children!
Kobayashi Issa

Marzana Day in Poland, celebrates the arrival of spring. ▶MCF.

Songs for spring. *See* pages 69 and 72.

21 March

Spring is beginning. The winter cold gives way to warmer weather. Each day is longer and each night shorter, and the sun climbs higher in the sky. All around us plants and trees begin new growth.

At such a time it is difficult to imagine that in some parts of the world it is now autumn. In New Zealand and Australia, for example, summer is over. Winter approaches, and the days grow shorter and cooler. The sun is lower in the sky.

When it is autumn here, in Britain, it will be spring in those countries.

Places like Kenya, right on the Equator, have very little change in their seasons. Even in December, when here we may have snows and blizzards, there they have burning heat, drying up the land. And as we now look forward to our warmer weather, Kenya eagerly awaits her rainy season, when much-needed rain will revive a parched landscape and fill the water-holes for thirsty animals.

In some countries where it is spring at the moment, people are also celebrating the beginning of a new year. Now, as plants start to grow and animals to breed, new year festivities are at the same time a celebration of new life in the earth at this season, and a happy welcome to the new year.

Poem for a rainy day

A good rain knows its season;
It comes at the edge of spring.
It steals through the night on the breeze
Noiselessly wetting everything.
Dark night, the clouds black as the roads,
Only a light on a boat gleaming.
In the morning, thoroughly soaked with water,
The flowers hang their heavy heads.
Spring Rain Tu Fu

Happiness

1 Spring is here at last;
   Dreary winter's past.
   Now the skies are ringing
   With the birds' loud singing.
   All the world is glad,
   Why should we be sad?
   Why should we be sad?

2 High above the earth,
   Filling Heaven with mirth,
   Larks their wings are beating,
   Men and angels greeting.
   All the world is glad,
   Why should we be sad?
   Why should we be sad?

3 You who stay below
   See Earth's beauty grow.
   Leave behind your sadness;
   Join our song of gladness.
   Banish care and fear,
   Happiness is here,
   Happiness is here.

►ECUS No 1

March

22 March

On this day in 1895, the cinema was born. Two brothers in France, Louis and Auguste Lumière, showed a short film, on a screen, to an audience. It was the first time this had ever been done.

Moving films had been invented some years earlier, but people had to look at them by peeping into a machine called a Kinetoscope. Only one person at a time could see the film this way.

It was the Lumière brothers who had the brilliant idea of projecting film onto a screen so that many people could view it at the same time. When they did this for the first time on March 22nd, their film lasted only 8 minutes, and showed workers leaving their factory for their dinner-hour.

But later that year they showed a film to a paying audience, and with this, the cinema had begun.

The following year a programme of films made by the Lumières was shown in Britain. One was called 'Arrival of a train at a station' and it thrilled the first British cinema audience with a shot of a train roaring straight towards the camera.

Other films shown were 'The Baby and the Goldfish', and 'The Family Teatable.' Of course these films had no sound-track, and were usually very short – nothing like the films we see now.

The new kind of entertainment fascinated people and quickly became very popular. Within a year of its beginnings in France, nearly every large country in Europe was showing films in cinemas.

There is a strange story about the first moving films ever made. They were taken about eight years earlier by another Frenchman, Louis Aimé Augustin Le Prince. He was on his way to demonstrate his invention in Paris. On September 16th he boarded a train. He never arrived. Neither he nor his equipment was ever seen again. The mystery remains unsolved to this day.

23 March

The birthday of Roger Bannister (born in 1929) who made sporting history by running the mile in under 4 minutes. *See* May 6th.

Easter

Easter is a very ancient spring festival. It was celebrated long before Christians chose it as a time to remember the story of Jesus Christ's death and rising from the dead.

The word Easter comes from the name of the ancient Saxon goddess of spring, Eostre (Eastre). The name means 'the dawn' and her festival was about the awakening of new life in the earth after winter.

When Christianity came to Britain, the celebration of Christ rising from the dead, and the ancient spring festival of Eostre were joined together and became one.

Some of the Easter traditions we still follow actually come from the ancient Saxon festival, although of course many of them have different meanings for Christians nowadays.

Chocolate eggs are quite a new custom. But for thousands of years people have used eggs to mean the new life which breaks from the earth in spring. In ancient China, Egypt, Greece, Persia, centuries before the first Easter day, people were making gifts of decorated eggs at spring festivals.

The Easter bunny who traditionally brings the Easter eggs comes from the hare, which was the sacred beast of the goddess Eostre.

Hot cross buns, traditionally eaten on Good Friday, have a long history. Ancient Greeks and Romans ate small cakes marked with a cross at spring festivals. So did the Saxons.

And so, like many other festivals celebrated in different parts of the world at this time of the year, Easter is at the same time a celebration of a religious story and a welcome to life in the earth after the gloom and cold of winter.

How we lost eleven days

Today was once New Year's day in this country. In fact, the year 1751 began on March 25th. The year 1752, however, began on January 1st, and the new year has begun on January 1st ever since.

In 1751 the calendar was not really working properly. The seasons were starting 11 days earlier than the calendar said they would. This was because the year is really shorter than the calendar year – 1 minute and 14 seconds shorter to be exact. But over hundreds of years, all these minutes and seconds had added up to 11 whole days.

So in 1751 Parliament decided to correct the mistake and make sure it couldn't happen again. They also had the problem of the 11 extra days. They had to get rid of them, somehow.

In September they decided simply to cross them off the calendar, as though they had never happened. One day it was September 3rd, and the next, Parliament announced, it was the 15th!

Obviously this caused some problems. Should people pay bills for those missing days? Had they happened, or had they not? Angry crowds gathered outside the king's palace and the Houses of Parliament, shouting 'Give us back our 11 days'. They lost the end of the year, too, because 1751 finished at the end of December so that the New Year could begin on January 1st.

Actually the calendar still isn't quite right. But after 4000 years, the mistake will only add up to 1¼ days, so we can be sure that no more correction will be needed for a very long time.

See also July page 100.

Passover

Just now Jewish people are celebrating Passover, the Feast of Unleavened Bread. This is the story they remember at this time:

Thousands of years ago, the Jews lived in Egypt. The Egyptian Pharaoh grew afraid of them. They were so many in number. Would they become too powerful, and join together with his enemies to fight against him?

He gave commands, that all the Jews be seized and set to labour under the merciless sun, as slaves. And he gave other orders too – that every newborn baby should be hurled into the River Nile to drown. This, he thought, would stop their numbers multiplying.

At this time, a Jewish child was born. The parents named him Moses. For a while they hid him safely. But when they could no longer do this, they made a floating basket of papyrus and placed him in it, hidden among the reeds beside the river bank.

There Pharaoh's daughter found him. She felt pity for the tiny child. She took him, and he became her son.

In time, Moses grew up. All around him he saw misery among his people. In sorrow he watched them, cowed by the harshness of their labour, bowed down beneath the cruelty of overseers who drove them ever harder, ever more brutally. One day a Jewish slave was beaten before his eyes. In anger, he killed the overseer, then fled Egypt to escape the punishment of angry Pharaoh.

Years passed. There came a time when God told Moses he had heard the cries of misery from Jews in Egypt. Moses must return as God's own messenger, to bring them out and lead them to another land.

So Moses did as he was asked. He travelled back to Egypt, and stood before the Pharaoh once again.

'Release the slaves,' he said. 'Allow them to come with me.'

Pharaoh refused. He did not want to lose their labour. He despised their God. He was not afraid of them.

But then God brought great suffering to punish the Egyptians and to show his power. Before their eyes, Moses struck the water of the River Nile, and it turned to blood, and stank. Blood appeared throughout the land in all the rivers and streams. There was no water anywhere.

The fields and cities teemed with frogs. They overran the homes, the ovens, the foodstores. They were even in the beds.

Each plague that came was more horrible than the one before. Gnats and flies swarmed over the land. Hailstorms beat down everything that grew. Locusts stripped the greenery from every living plant and tree.

Then came the most terrible punishment of all. Every first-born Egyptian son would die.

Moses told each Jewish family to kill a lamb and smear its blood around the doorway of their homes. For, God told Moses, the Angel of Death would see the blood, and would pass over in the night. But in every Egyptian home the eldest son died. There was great grief and sorrow throughout the land.

In terror now, the Egyptians pleaded with Moses to depart and take his people out.

The Jews prepared. They ate a special meal: lamb, and bread without yeast, and bitter herbs. Early the next morning they set out, and so began their long journey through the deserts to a promised land.

This is the story of the first Passover. It is told every year when the festival is celebrated in the spring. And special foods are eaten: unleavened bread (bread without yeast), in memory of the haste in which they left Egypt; lamb to show God's power in saving them from the Angel of Death on Passover night; bitter herbs in memory of the misery of slavery; green vegetables, a sign of life, to show how God provided food and water on their journey through the desert; and *charoset*, a mixture of fruit, nuts, wine and spices, to show the sweetness of freedom. Lastly an egg, the symbol of new life for the people leaving slavery behind them.

31 March

Oranges and Lemons ceremony in London. ▶ MCF.

The seasons of the year

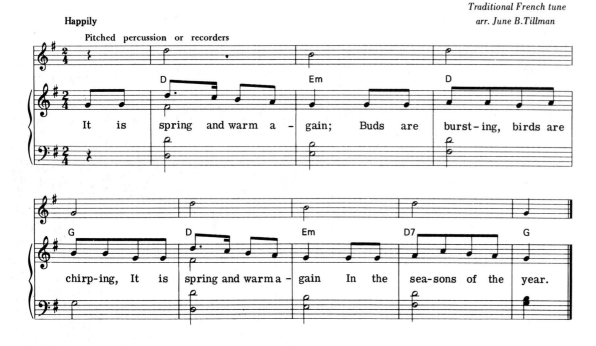

Traditional French tune
arr. June B. Tillman

1   It is spring and warm again;
Buds are bursting,
Birds are chirping,
It is spring and warm again
In the seasons of the year.

2   It is summertime again;
Sun is shining,
Fruit is ripening,
It is summertime again
In the seasons of the year.

3   It is autumn once again;
Leaves are turning,
Bonfires burning,
It is autumn once again
In the seasons of the year.

4   Winter days are here again;
Frost is nipping,
Feet are slipping,
Winter days are here again
In the seasons of the year.

**(You can sing this song at any time of
the year, starting with the
appropriate verse for the season.)**

▶ECUS No 6

April

In some years the following festivals may fall in April:

Easter falls between March 22nd and April 24th. *See* page 70 and song on page 77. ▶ MCF and F&F.

Mothering Sunday falls between March 4th and April 7th. ▶ MCF. *See* Class Assembly page 121.

Passover. *See* March page 71. ▶ F&F.

Ramadan. ▶ MCF. *See also* Night of Power, June page 93.

April's name

This month gets its name from the month of *Aprilis* in the ancient Roman calendar. No one is really certain what it means. Some say that it comes from the Latin word *aperire,* which means 'to open', because it is a time when plant buds are opening with the arrival of the spring in the northern half of the world.

The Romans dedicated their month of *Aprilis* to the goddess Venus, who watched over the sowing of seeds and the planting of young crops, protecting and nurturing the new growth of these early spring days.

Signs of spring

> See! The Winter is past;
> the rains are over and gone.
> Flowers appear on the earth;
> the season of singing has come.
> The cooing of doves
> is heard in our land.
> The fig-tree forms its early fruit;
> the blossoming vines spread their fragrance.
> *Song of Songs*

2 April

Today is the birthday of Hans Christian Andersen (born 1805), who wrote many famous tales loved by people of all ages. Here is part of his story *The Ugly Duckling*. It is supposed to be about his own life. It tells of an ugly duckling driven from his family because he is so ugly. Laughed at and scorned by everyone, he goes on his travels. He comes to a hovel, in which an old woman lives with a cat and a hen . . .

'The cat was the master of the house and the hen the mistress; they were always saying, 'We and the world,' for they looked on themselves as half the world, and the better half at that. The duckling thought that there might be other opinions on that matter, but the hen would not hear of it.

'Can you lay eggs?' she asked. 'No? Then kindly keep your views to yourself!'

The cat asked, 'Can you arch your back and purr, or give out sparks? No? Then you had better keep quiet while sensible people are talking.'

So the duckling sat in a corner and moped. Thoughts of fresh air and sunshine came into his mind; and then, an extraordinary longing seized him to float on the water. At last, he could not help telling the hen about it.

'What a preposterous notion!' she exclaimed. 'The trouble with you is that you have nothing to do; that's why you get these fancies. Just lay a few eggs, or practise purring, and they'll pass off.'

'But it is so delicious to float on the water,' said the duckling. 'It is so lovely to put down your head and dive to the bottom.'

'That *must* be delightful!' said the hen sarcastically. 'You must be out of your mind! Ask the cat – he's the cleverest person I know – if *he* likes floating on the water, or diving to the bottom. Never mind my opinion: ask our mistress, the old

woman; there's no one wiser in the whole world. Do you imagine that *she* wants to float or put her head under water?'

'You don't understand,' said the duckling, sadly.

'Well, if we don't understand you, nobody will. You'll never be as wise as the cat and the old woman, to say nothing of myself. Don't give yourself airs, child, but be thankful for all the good things that have been done for you. Haven't you found a warm room and elegant company, from whom you can learn plenty if you listen? But all you do is talk nonsense; you're not even cheerful to be with. Believe me, I mean this for your own good. Now do make an effort to lay some eggs, or at least learn to purr and give out sparks.'

'I think I had better go out into the wide world,' said the duckling.

'All right, do,' said the hen.

So the duckling went. He floated on the water,

April

and dived below the surface; but it seemed to him that other ducks ignored him because of his ugliness . . .

One evening, as the sky flamed with the setting sun, a flock of marvellous great birds rose out of the rushes. The duckling had never seen any birds so beautiful. They were brilliantly white, with long graceful necks – indeed, they were swans; uttering a strange sound, they spread their splendid wings and flew far away to warmer lands and lakes which did not freeze. High in the air they soared, and the ugly duckling was filled with a wild excitement; he turned round and round in the water like a wheel, and called out in a voice so loud and strange that it quite frightened him. Oh, he would never forget those wonderful birds, those fortunate birds! As soon as the last was out of sight, he dived right down to the bottom of the water, and when he came up again he was almost frantic. He did not know what the birds were called; he did not know where they had come from, nor where they were flying – but he felt more deeply drawn to them than to anything he had ever known.

The winter grew colder still. The duckling had to swim round and round in the water to keep it from freezing over; but every night the ice-free part became smaller. Then he had to use his feet all the time to break up the surface: at last, however, he was quite worn out . . .

But it would be too sad to tell you of all the hardships and miseries that he had to go through during that cruel winter. One day he was huddling among the reeds in the marsh when the sun began to send down warm rays again; the larks started their song; how glorious! It was spring. The duckling raised his wings. They seemed stronger than before, and carried him swiftly away; before he realized what was happening, he was in a lovely garden full of apple-trees in blossom, and where

sweet-smelling lilac hung on its long boughs right down to the winding stream. And then, directly in front of him, out of the leafy shadows, came three magnificent white swans, ruffling their feathers as they floated lightly over the water. The duckling recognised the wonderful birds, and a strange sadness came over him.

'I will fly to those noble birds, even though they may peck me to death for daring to come near them, an ugly thing like me. But I don't care – better to be killed by such splendid creatures than to be pecked by ducks and hens and kicked by the poultry-yard girl – or be left to suffer another winter like the last.' So he flew out to the open water, and swam towards the glorious swans. They saw him, and came speeding towards him, ruffling their plumage.

'Yes, kill me,' said the poor creature, bowing his head right down to the water as he waited for his end. Yet what did he see reflected below? He beheld his own likeness – but he was no longer an awkward ugly dark grey bird. He was like the proud white birds about him; he was a swan.

It doesn't matter if you are born in a duck-yard, so long as you come from a swan's egg.'

The Ugly Duckling Hans Christian Andersen

5 April

About 120 years ago, having an operation in hospital was a very dangerous business. More than half the patients died from blood-poisoning – that is, their surgery wounds became infected, and the infection reached the blood.

At this time, hospitals were probably the most unhealthy places you could be if you were sick. People died, not from the illnesses which had brought them there, but from infections from the millions of germs in wards and operating theatres.

Doctors and nurses knew nothing about these dangers. Operating theatres and instruments were very dirty. Surgeons wore their ordinary clothes to do the operation, just as they had come in off the streets. They went from one patient to another, unaware of the quantities of killer germs they carried with them.

There was an English doctor, Joseph Lister, working in a hospital in Scotland, who was determined to do something about these deaths. He was appalled at the number of his own patients he was losing. They always seemed to be getting better after he had operated on them. But on the fourth day, their wounds became infected, and a short while later, they would die.

One day, he read something which gave him an idea. In France, a scientist named Louis Pasteur had found that it was germs that caused infection and decay. His ideas had not been fully proved. But Lister thought they made a lot of sense. He remembered seeing something called carbolic acid poured o rubbish to kill the smell. The smell, he knew, was caused by the rubbish decaying. Would carbolic acid also work on germs on human beings?

He tried it for the first time in 1865. To his distress, the man still died. He realised that the patient had been far too ill already for the experiment to work. A few months later he tried it again. He and his assistant, James McPhee, put a carbolic dressing on the wound on a young boy's leg.

Then they waited to see if it would work.

Three days passed. On the fourth, the boy complained of pain. Lister took the dressing off. The wound was healthy. Only the carbolic had been too strong, and burned the skin a little.

So the experiment had worked. Lister began using carbolic throughout his hospital to kill the germs, and he taught everyone who worked with him to do the same. Once, at least fifty out of every hundred patients died. Now it was only three in every hundred.

It was some time before surgeons in other hospitals accepted Lister's discovery and begun to use it. But in the end they did. The age of antiseptics, the name for carbolic and other germ-killers like it, had begun.

On this day, Lister's birthday (he was born in 1827), we should remember the beginning of antiseptics in our hospitals, and also all the other ways in which he taught us to keep hospitals and equipment free from germs. It is something that we take for granted now for very few people die from infections after operations. We have Joseph Lister to thank for that.

See also August 15th, September 28th, November 15th.

9 April

Today is the birthday of a man remembered for his remarkable and inventive achievements, his enormous energy and imagination. He was Isambard Kingdom Brunel, the engineer who designed and built the railway from London to the south-west of Britain, crossing hills and deep wooded valleys with hundreds of tunnels and bridges. He was born in 1806.

One of his first projects was the Clifton Suspension Bridge. There is a story of how he had himself swung out in a basket across the Clifton Gorge, hundreds of feet above the ground, hanging by a rope from an iron bar on a roller. Some way across, the roller jammed. Brunel simply climbed out of the basket, shinned up the rope, and freed it.

He was a dedicated and painstaking workman. His plan drawings were filled with fine, minute details. He watched over the building of every part of his projects with tremendous care. While working on the Great Western Railway – from London to Bristol and then on into Devon and Cornwall – he travelled continually up and down the line in a special coach containing everything he needed to continue working all the time.

Brunel also designed and built three of the first great steamships. His first, the *Great Western*, was also the first steamship to make regular crossings of the Atlantic. His second, the *Great Britain*, was the first of the great luxury passenger liners making that crossing. Certainly its passengers thought it was sumptuous, although the Ship's Rules for Passengers show that life on board was rather different from that of a luxury liner today!

'Every passenger to rise at 7am unless otherwise permitted by the surgeon.

The passengers, when dressed, to roll up their beds, to sweep the decks, (including the space under the bottom of the berths), and to throw the dirt overboard.

Breakfast not to commence till this is done.

The occupant of each berth to see his own berth is well brushed out; and single women are to keep their own compartment tidy.

The beds to be well shaken and aired on deck.'

Brunel's last ship was the giant *Great Eastern*, which was 210 metres long. Tragically, Brunel fell ill just before she sailed on her first voyage. He died a week later. But he might have been pleased to know that she lived up to the scale of his achievements.

Up to this time, the only way for news to cross the oceans was by ship, for this was many years before radio or telephones had been invented. Brunel's *Great Eastern* changed all that, for she laid the first transatlantic telegraph cable and other underwater telegraph cables around the world. And so she opened a new era in the building of links between the continents, and helped to create the first means by which news could be carried fast across the great stretches of water which separate the land masses of the world.

See also August page 7, September 15th.

13 April

Baisakhi. At this festival in CE 1699 Guru Gobind Singh formed the Khalsa, the brotherhood of Sikhs.

See Guru Gobind Singh's Birthday. December page 43. ▶F&F.

14 April

On a dark, cold night in 1912, just after midnight, the largest and most luxurious ship that had ever been built was steaming through the Atlantic. It was her first voyage. She had all the best equipment on board, and she was built in the most up-to-date way. She was believed to be unsinkable.

Earlier, another ship had warned her that icebergs were in the area. Confidently, and unworried, the Titanic steamed on.

When the iceberg loomed suddenly in her path, she had no time to avoid it. The great ice mountain ripped into her hull, flooding her with water. Front first, slowly the gigantic, unsinkable boat began to slide below the waves.

At first everyone was calm. In an orderly way, passengers climbed into the lifeboats, women and children first. The ship tilted a bit more, and then slid deeper into the black, freezing water.

Then the full horror struck them. There were not enough lifeboats. By the time the rescue ship arrived, the Titanic had disappeared beneath the sea, with more than 1500 people drowned. Only about 700 were still alive.

Those who survived owed their lives to one thing. Before the Titanic went down, she had sent radio messages for help, and these were heard by another ship.

Radio, or wireless as it was known then, was very new. Many ships did not have it. If they did, there were not enough operators, so that there were many hours while they slept and there was no one to hear the messages.

So many had been rescued on the Titanic

because of the radio, that it convinced the world that all ships should have one, and that it should be used day and night.

In fact, the ship that had first warned the Titanic of icebergs was near enough to have saved every person on board. But while the Titanic went down, the other ship's exhausted radio operator had been fast asleep. The ship's crew had not even known the Titanic was in trouble.

Two other important things happened after the Titanic's tragedy. An international ice watch began, with special ships to check for icebergs and send warnings to other ships. And new laws were passed, making ship's owners supply their ships with enough lifeboats to provide at least one place for everyone on board.

What a tragedy that it took the doomed voyage of the SS Titanic, and the deaths of so many, before people demanded that shipowners should make their ships safer!

See also December 12th.

It's Easter

Words by Winifred E. Styles
Music by G. F. Root

1 Bells are ringing, bells are ringing for
   Easter, for Easter,
   Children singing, children singing for
      glad Easter-time.
   Alleluia! Alleluia! It's Easter, It's Easter!
   Alleluia! Alleluia! It's glad Easter-time.

2 Flowers growing, flowers growing for
   Easter, for Easter,
   Breezes blowing, breezes blowing for glad
      Easter-time.
   Alleluia! Alleluia! etc.

3 Carols singing, carols singing for Easter,
   for Easter,
   Praises bringing, praises bringing for glad
      Easter-time.
   Alleluia! Alleluia! etc.

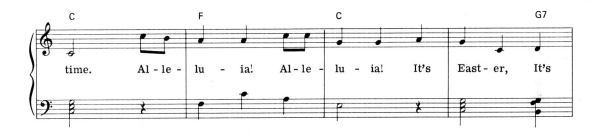

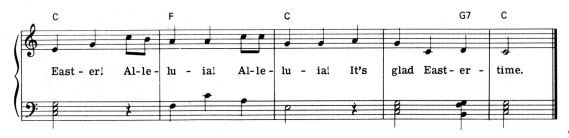

▶ MCF page 37

77

April

The coming of the rains

In some parts of the world, people are now eagerly awaiting rain after long months of dry and burning heat. Without the rain, crops will fail and animals go short of water. And without crops and animals, there is no food for anyone to eat.

People tell stories about the coming of the rains, and their life-giving powers. Here is one story from Madagascar, a large island far out in the Indian Ocean.

The land was empty, burned by the sun, barren, brown. There was no living thing on it, no plant or tree.

From high in the clouds, the god Driana-nahary looked down, and wondered. Was there anything that could live in that vast wasteland of sand and rock. Could anything survive that heat? He wondered, and he wondered, until he resolved to wonder no more.

He called his son. And pointing to the land appearing and disappearing in the gap between the drifting clouds, he said, 'I have a task for you. Go down and find out what the earth is like. See if anything can live on it. But don't stay long. Be fast in going, and return at once.'

His son, Atoko-loinona was pleased with the request. He too had often peered between the clouds and wondered what the distant land was like. So, losing no time, he dropped from the airy heavens and fell to earth.

At once, he felt the blast of heat above the surface of the land, like a wall through which he had to pass. And when he landed it was on dry desert sand. As far as the eye could see, to north and south, to east and west, there was the sand and rock, and nothing else. No shelter from the burn of the sun. No living plant. Of life-giving water, he could not see a single drop.

The answer for his father was a simple one. He must return at once and tell him that nothing could survive this land.

He climbed a sandy slope, to make his leap up into the clouds. They looked so cool and welcoming, yet at that moment they seemed further away than they had ever been. The heat dragged at his limbs, like chains to hold him back. He summoned all his strength, and leapt . . . and only fell down on his hands and knees. He could not fly! He tried again. Again he failed. Each leap became more desperate. Each time he landed on the desert floor.

Now he was certain he would die, unless he found shelter soon. Each minute he was weaker, his lips now parched and cracked with thirst, his eyes blurred with the white hot glare . . .

He fell to the ground. Then, summoning all his remaining strength, he scooped a tunnel in the sand, half crawling, half falling into it, to escape the murderous rays above.

The god Driana-nahary was becoming anxious. In the gathering gloom of dusk, Atoko had not returned. Throughout the night he watched the silent earth. No one appeared.

So now, he must act swiftly to save his son. In that very instant, as he thought of it, he created the first living beings, people, and he set them on earth to search in every direction for the missing boy.

Northwards they moved, and to the south, the east, the west, a great army moving, searching, moving everywhere. There was only the barren surface staring bleakly back at them.

And they too began to wither in the heat. Thirst, and then hunger sapped their strength. Their limbs became like leaden weights. One by one they sank to the ground, and lay there motionless.

Driana-nahary saw them. He *must* not lose them, as he had lost his son. And with a mighty blow he struck the clouds. Lightning sparked across the earth, and thunder boomed, and from the clouds the rain burst forth and poured in torrents on the thirsty earth below . . .

The people stirred. They raised their heads. They lifted up their hands, and caught the rain, and drank. Then they began to dance – a wild joyous dance that spoke of thanks and life renewed and celebration. As the raindrops seeped into the earth about them, the soil, transformed, grew rich and black and moist. Plants and trees burst from it, flowers bloomed. The empty barrenness became a paradise of green.

Here they settled, learned to till and cultivate the soil, had children, multiplied and prospered.

Atoko was never seen again. Driana-nahary for ever sorrowed that he had lost his son.

And yet he had much to occupy his love, for were there not his people on the earth, for him to care for and preserve, and guide in their new life?

19 April
Charles Darwin died in 1882. *See* January page 51.

23 April
Today is St George's day, the feast day of the patron saint of England, Portugal, Germany, Aragon (in Spain) and the cities of Genoa and Venice, in Italy.

St George was a Christian put to death for his beliefs somewhere between 1600 and 1700 years ago. He may have been a soldier in the Roman army. But these few facts are really all we know about the real St George.

Most of what we hear about him is legend. It began about 900 years after he lived, when soldiers returning from the Crusades brought back the tales.

Here is one story. It tells how St George put faith in God and found enormous strength and courage.

The cold light of dawn stole through the misty streets, across the shuttered houses. Silence and terror hung like a cloak of dark despair about the city. The people crept from their houses, grey-faced, to gather in the market square.

Today, the last and final victim would go to her death – the king's own daughter. Together they would lead her to the lake, where in the shallows the monster lurked.

For months their city had been no more than a feeding ground. Each dawn the monstrous beast surged upwards and seized its prey – the sons and daughters of the town. There was no longer any laughter in the streets. No children playing games, no sound of youthful voices filled the air.

The bravest of the city had ridden out to kill it. Every one had fallen to the deadly jaws.

Today, the last, the Princess would feed the beast. By the lakeside the people gathered round. Their sorrow brought an icy stillness to the air. They knew her death would bring no freedom for them. Nor had the other deaths before. The beast would feed and feed – and when would it ever end?

Then, on the shores, a horse appeared and drew near to them. Its rider enquired what caused their weeping misery. It was St George, and he had seen them watch the shallows of the lake with terror in their eyes.

He heard their story. At once he fell onto his knees, and prayed that God would give him strength and courage to defy the beast and save the city from its monstrous hold.

And as he did so, the ground began to tremble, and the stench of evil filled the air, of slime and dank, black rancid water. Upwards the dragon rose, belching and fuming with the blood of victims.

The people fled. Alone, the girl and knight stood firm. 'My life is over,' the girl told him. 'Save yours. Flee to the city, now.'

For answer, St George bent down and seized a stone. With all his strength he flung it in the monster's face. In shock, the great beast swayed into the air, then hissed in rage and snaked its scaly neck towards him. He raised his foot and stamped it down, pinning the neck against the mud. Then taking the princess's belt, praying all the time, he bound it tightly round the head and jaws.

In the city, the people awaited fearfully. For a long time they saw nothing. Then, along the stony road towards the city gate, they saw the knight, and then the girl, and then the dragon, docile, like a pet led calmly by the young girl's hand.

In disbelief they stared. And then with one mighty roar of joy and wonder and relief, they surged through the gates towards the conquering knight.

And so evil is defeated by the power of good once more – a theme of many stories which are told at this time of year, when spring conquers winter and the summer warmth begins.

23 April
Children's Day in Turkey. ▶ MCF.

Escape from the floods

April can be a time of heavy rain in Europe, and sometimes floods. Here is part of a story set in France. When the River Loire bursts its banks and floods the valley, a school is cut off from the outer world. Nervously, teachers and pupils watch the waters rise around them. Desperately, they build a dam across the gateway to the school, using soil and gravel from their games fields.

But then the garden walls cave in, and flood water gushes in. At last, they decide to evacuate as fast as possible. Some leave in vans along what little is left of the main road. The last few pupils, and one teacher, wait for the vehicle to return and pick them up . . .

'Five minutes passed, then ten, then a quarter of an hour. It was growing darker and darker. A distant rumble rolled across the floods. It was not thunder. There had been no lightning flash to herald the mighty murmur that boomed above the waters. There was still no sign of Monsieur Juillet's blue van at the end of that mile and a half of road which emerged from the waterlogged fields. And soon there was no road.

In the twinkling of an eye it had disappeared as though by magic. Monsieur Sala was the first to notice and he shouted to warn the others. The waters of the Loire were pouring down in a tidal wave two miles wide which fanned out in foam and a whirl of wreckage.

They shot through the gate, sprinted along the duckboards and dived into the nearest building.

'Upstairs!' Monsieur Sala bellowed, chivvying and chasing the laggards.

Only when they reached the first floor did they pause for breath. Some dared to look out of the window. A muddy sea billowed down the drive, poured through the gate like a mill-race, foamed against walls and trees, shivered windows and made matchwood of doors, and flooded gurgling into buildings. Nothing could stop it as it crashed on and filled the courtyard with a deafening din.

Then the thunder of the waves grew gradually less, fell away and died in the inexhaustible murmur of the pouring rain.

Monsieur Sala had run to one of the front windows to watch the waters do their worst. At last, and only when he had seen the flood reach its peak midway between ground and first floor, did he come out on the landing and count those who remained.

There were seven, himself included . . . The main thing was that they were alive. Their business now was to organize things so that they should remain so for the next four or five days . . . Monsieur Sala took Vignoles and Charpenne to one side. He lowered his voice.

'We're not going to let ourselves be drowned here. How do we know that the water won't be up to this floor by tomorrow? We must build a raft with whatever we can scrape together and be ready to escape when the moment comes' . . .

Job Trévidic was already rummaging in the attics overhead for anything that would float. Unfortunately, in view of the number of passengers and the scantiness of the material at their disposal, it soon became clear that they would have to build not one, but two rafts.

The first was finished in four hours. To a base of two wooden bed-frames a miscellaneous collection of chair seats, tins, old tubs and planks torn from the dormitory partitioning was lashed with wire and sheets plaited into ropes. They carried it downstairs to the gloomy patch of water that filled the hall. Job volunteered to test it. As soon as he stepped aboard it lurched and tipped its captain overboard. The Breton pulled himself out of his cold bath by clutching the banisters and stood, dripping wet and furious. He made a second and less energetic attempt and called to Picard and Vignoles. With three aboard her the raft floated after a fashion, provided her passengers lay on their stomachs and kept still.

They went straight on with the second. At first Boisson de Chazelles had dodged the work, but now he was co-operative and lent all the help he could. Exploring the bathrooms, his was the bright idea of unfixing the hot-water tanks. These they emptied and replugged and then used as floatation chambers on the new raft. All that was necessary was to lash a whole pitch-pine partition securely over them When they tested it, the new raft proved the better of the two. It could carry four people with sufficient free-board.'

Flood Warning Paul Berna

This, of course, is not nearly the end of their adventures. And when it is all over, they have all learned a great deal. Each discovers unexpected bravery, imagination and ideas to help himself and the others live through the ordeal. The youngest and the oldest, the quietest and shyest, and the most loud and boisterous – each one helps in some particular way. And in the end, they all survive. *See also* June page 98.

25 April
Guglielmo Marconi, inventor of the radio, was born in 1874. *See* December 12th.

26 April
About 420 years ago today (1564), a baby was christened in a church in Stratford-upon-Avon, England. The baby was William Shakespeare, whose plays have delighted theatregoers in every century since he lived. His stories still have the same power to capture the imagination as when he wrote them about 400 years ago.

We actually know very little about Shakespeare himself. Finding out is a bit like a detective story – small clues have to be put together and guesses made from what we know about life in England at that time.

We do know that by the time he was 28 he was already a well-known and popular actor and writer, working in London with the best acting company of the time.

They often acted at the Court of Queen Elizabeth I, presenting plays which Shakespeare wrote for the occasion. They also played to noblemen and their friends and followers, who gathered at each other's wealthy homes.

The plays Shakespeare wrote for these kinds of audiences were light-hearted tales of mystery and surprise, always with happy endings. They were designed to amuse and enchant the audience, to delight them with their elegance and charm. They are such plays as Midsummer's Night Dream, Twelfth Night, The Taming of the Shrew.

But Shakespeare's main audiences were the people of London – the boisterous crowds of law students and young apprentices learning a trade, the fine ladies and gentlemen of fashion, the wealthy merchants and the tradesmen of the city. And there were always the noblemen, with their great trains of followers. Here, in the public theatres, to the joyful chorus of clapping, booing and hissing as the excitement of each story mounted, Shakespeare learned his skills as actor and writer. For these energetic audiences, he wrote most of his plays, and here he made his name as an exciting and dramatic playwright.

Elizabethans loved plays about the history of England and its past kings. Shakespeare wrote a number of these. Most of them were for the enjoyment of a few noblemen in particular who were soldiers themselves. Some of the best known plays of this kind are Richard II and Richard III, King John, Henry IV and Henry V.

His most famous plays are ones he wrote towards the end of his work. They are known as the tragedies – plays such as Macbeth, Othello, Hamlet, King Lear and Julius Caesar. These are the ones most often performed nowadays, often because they explore ideas which audiences still find interesting.

Shakespeare died in 1616. Every century since then, his plays have been performed. In some countries there are special theatres for presenting them – Britain, for example has a Royal Shakespeare Theatre in Stratford. It holds a Shakespeare festival there every year.

'He was not for an age, but for all time,'said Ben Johnson, one of Shakespeare's friends and another important writer of the time. For Shakespeare may be dead, but his work will be very much alive, as long as there are actors to bring his plays to life, and audiences to be enthralled by them.

April

Poem for a windy day

The wind one morning sprang up from sleep,
Saying, 'Now for a frolic! now for a leap!
Now for a madcap galloping chase!
I'll make a commotion in every place!'

So it swept with a bustle right through a great
    town,
Cracking the signs and scattering down
Shutters; and whisking with merciless
    squalls,
Old women's bonnets and gingerbread stalls.

There never was heard a much lustier shout,
As the apples and oranges trundled about;
And the urchins that stand, with their
    thievish eyes
For ever on watch, ran off each with a prize.

Then away to the fields it went blustering and
    humming,
And the cattle all wondered what monster
    was coming.
It plucked by the tails the grave matronly
    cows,
And tossed the colts' manes all over their
    brows;
Till, offended at such an unusual salute,
They all turned their backs and stood sulky
    and mute.

So on it went, capering and playing its
    pranks —
Whistling with reeds on the broad river's
    banks,
Puffing the birds as they sat on the spray,
Or the traveller grave on the King's highway.
It was not too nice to hustle the bags
Of the beggar, and flutter his dirty rags;
'Twas so bold that it feared not to play its
    joke
With the doctor's wig or the gentleman's
    cloak.

Through the forest it roared, and cried gaily,
    'Now,
You sturdy old oaks, I'll make you bow!'
And it made them bow without more ado,
For it cracked their great branches through
    and through.

Then it rushed like a monster on cottage and
    farm,
Striking their dwellers with sudden alarm;
And they ran out like bees in a mid-summer
    swarm;
There were dames with their kerchiefs tied
    over their caps,
To see if their poultry were free from
    mishaps;

The turkeys they gobbled, the geese screamed
    aloud,
And the hens crept to roost in a terrified
    crowd;
There was rearing of ladders, and logs were
    laid on,
Where the thatch from the roof threatened
    soon to be gone.

But the wind had swept on, and had met in a
    lane
With a schoolboy, who panted and struggled
    in vain;
For it tossed him and twirled him, then
    passed — and he stood
With his hat in a pool, and shoes in the mud!

Then away went the wind in its holiday glee,
And now it was far on the billowy sea:
And the lordly ships felt its staggering blow,
And the little boats darted to and fro.

But, lo! it was night, and it sank to rest
On the sea-bird's rock in the gleaming west,
Laughing to think, in its frolicsome fun,
How little of mischief it really had done.

The Wind in a Frolic William Howitt

Bran Tub
30p

Summer Term

May

In some years the following festivals may fall in May:

Ascension Day Christian festival. Celebrates Jesus going up into Heaven and his last appearance to his disciples. Comes 40 days after Easter.

Martyrdom of Guru Arjan Dev Sikh festival. ▶F&F.

Ramadan. ▶MCF. *See* Night of Power, June page 93. **Eid-ul-Fitr** celebrates the end of Ramadan. ▶F&F.

Rogationtide. ▶MCF.

Shavout Jewish festival commemorating the giving of the Ten Commandments to Moses. It comes seven weeks after Pesach.

Wesak Buddhist Festival. *See* page 89. ▶F&F.

Whitsun. ▶F&F.

May's name

The month of May is named after Maia, the Roman Earth Mother, mother of the fertile soil, whom they believed brought forth new growth in spring.

The Greeks also had a goddess named Maia, and the Romans often confused her with their own. She was one of the daughters of the Greek god, Atlas, and there is a legend that she and her sisters were being pursued across the mountains by the hunter Orion. As he drew closer to them, they called to Zeus, lord of the gods, for help, Zeus heard their plea, and turned them into doves, then placed them in the sky as stars.

These are the stars which appear in the sky in the middle of May, heralding the arrival of good weather.

And so Maia the Earth Mother, and Maia the star who tells of summer weather are both fitting names for this fifth month of the year when we look forward to warmer days.

1 May

May Day or Labour Day in many countries of the world. ▶MCF.

5 May

It was just after 8 o'clock on the morning of May 5th, 1930. A handful of people watched a tiny aircraft climb from a runway of Croydon Airport, England, and rise towards the clouds above the English Channel.

That little plane was soaring into the first stage of a 16,000km journey that would take it southeast across the land masses of Europe, Asia, southeast Asia, and on to the shores of Australia.

The pilot was a young woman, Amy Johnson. When she landed at Port Darwin in Australia 19½ days later, she had become the first woman to fly solo – alone – in an aeroplane to Australia.

Yet she had only started to fly a mere 18 months earlier! The longest distance she had ever flown before was 320km (200miles). She started flying when she was working as a secretary in London, saving enough money from her wages to pay for flying lessons once a fortnight. Less than a year later, she had her pilot's licence. Later she also qualified as a ground engineer and a navigator.

Now she was embarking on a flight in which she would be alone in the air from sunrise to nightfall. During every second in the air, she would have to concentrate both on navigating and flying the aeroplane. Each night there would be very little sleep and many hours servicing and checking the plane for the following day's flight.

It was an eventful journey. Sandstorms stalled the aeroplane's engine, and forced her down into the desert. Her wing collided with a building as she fought a headwind on landing at another place. She battled through torrential rains and vicious winds of monsoon storms. Even her landing gear collapsed on one occasion, just as she touched down. By the time the journey was over, she was using sticking plaster on the little plane's wings, they had been repaired so often.

On May 24th she landed in Australia to an ecstatic welcome. People wrote songs and poems about her flight. And in Britain, nearly 200,000 people gathered to greet her on her return.

Tragically, Amy Johnson disappeared 11 years later, when she was ferrying an aircraft during the Second World War. She is believed to have gone into the sea off the English coast.

But the woman who had been determined to show that she, and others like her, could be just as skilled at flying as any man, had certainly done so, and her name has gone down in history for that.

5 May

Boy's Festival in Japan. ▶MCF.

6 May

No one could run a mile in less than 4 minutes, or so everyone thought, thirty years ago. For nine years the world record had been 4 minutes, 1.3 seconds, and this was believed to be just about as fast as it could be done.

But everyone was proved wrong. On this day in 1954, a British athlete named Roger Bannister ran a mile in only 3 minutes 59.4 seconds.

Bannister trained in a special way to achieve his running speed, for he made a study of how the human body moves and worked out the most efficient way to run fast. With that, and with the help of his friends Christopher Chataway and Christopher Brasher who ran with him, he broke the world record for the first time in nine years. And, almost more important than that, he crossed that formerly impassable four-minute barrier. Now athletes think little of running a mile in less than four minutes – and the world record is [3.46] minutes.

6 May

Following the introduction of the Penny Post, the first postage stamps were put on sale in 1840. *See* January 10th.

How Old-Spider made the world

This story about the creation of the world comes from the tiny island of Nauru in the Pacific Ocean. It shows how closely the life of island people is bound up with the sea and all its creatures. Stories a little like this are told on many other Pacific islands.

There was a time when there was nothing but the sea. Above it, Old-Spider hovered, ready for the time when she would make the world. There came a day on which she found a giant clam, an enormous shellfish with its shell close fastened against her. In vain she tried to probe an opening. When she tapped, there was a hollow, empty sound. Speaking the magic words which only Old-Spider knew, she opened the shell a little and passed inside.

All was darkness in there. The space was narrow, so she had to crouch. She searched and searched until she found what she was looking for – a snail. She clasped the creature to her, and sank into a deep, peaceful sleep. For three days she stayed like this, and all the while the snail drew from her body all the powers it would need to help her make the world.

Old-Spider woke. Again she searched until she found another, larger snail. She took the creature up, slept as before, and woke.

The work could now begin.

She said to one, 'Open this room a little,' and it did. Then she took the snail and fastened it in the upper shell to become the moon.

By its light she saw Rigi, the eel. 'Help me open up this room a little more,' she said. He pushed upwards, pressing with all his might, until he had wrenched the clam shell far apart. From his straining body, salt waters flowed and collected in the shell, and became the sea.

A little more pushing, and he had lifted the upper shell so high that it became the sky.

From the second, larger snail, Old-Spider made the sun. The lower shell became the earth.

And at last the work was finished. Earth and sky and sun and moon and all the waters of the sea were made.

See also January 28th, October page 26.

11 May

In 1897 Marconi sent his first wireless message across water. *See* December 12th.

A bumpy ride

It is difficult to imagine what travelling must have been like a few hundred years ago, before there were proper roads, and certainly no cars or railways.

The only means of transport was a horsedrawn vehicle, on roads which were often just about impassable.

Most of them were no more than a couple of ditches dug on either side of a track. The soil from the ditches was tossed into the centre, in the hopes that traffic would flatten it. More often, it became a sea of oozing mud. Horses sank up to their bellies. Or there were ruts, often over a metre deep, that would rattle a passenger half to death.

People travelled only by day, so that they could see the dangers ahead of them. And there were other hazards if you travelled after dark – the many highwaymen who preyed upon the travellers and robbed them.

Stage coaches were very slow compared with the speed of traffic nowadays. At most they covered five or six kilometres an hour, possibly 64 kilometres a day. But even this was a bone-shaking experience, as is shown by this account from a German visitor 200 years ago. (The 'basket' he talks of was at the back of the coach and held the luggage.)

'I must observe,' he writes, 'that (the English) have here a curious way of riding, not in, but upon, a stage coach. Persons to whom it is not convenient to pay a full price, instead of the inside, sit on the top of the coach, without any seats or even a rail. By what means passengers thus fasten themselves securely on the roof of these vehicles, I know not; but you constantly see numbers seated there, apparently at their ease, and in perfect safety.

May

This they call riding on the outside, for which they pay only half as much as those pay who are within. We had at present six of those passengers over our heads, who, when we alighted, frequently made such a noise and bustle as sometimes almost frightened us.

He who can properly balance himself rides not incommodiously on the outside. And in the summer time, in fine weather, on account of the prospects, it certainly is more pleasant than it is within; excepting that the company is generally low, and the dust is likewise more troublesome than in the inside, where at any rate you may draw up the windows according to your pleasure.

The inside passengers got in, in the yard, but we on the outside were obliged to clamber up in the public street because we should have had no room for our heads to pass under the gateway . . .

The getting up alone was at the risk of one's neck; and when I was up I was obliged to sit just at the corner of the coach, with nothing to hold by but a sort of little handle, fastened on the side. I sat nearest the wheel, and the moment that we set off I fancied I saw certain death await me. All I could do was to take still faster hold of the handle, and to be more and more careful to preserve my balance.

The machine now rolled along with prodigious rapidity, over the stones through the town, and every moment we seemed to fly into the air; so that it was almost a miracle that we still stuck to the coach and did not fall. We seemed to be thus on the wing, and to fly, as often as we passed through a village or went down a hill.

At last, the being continually in fear of my life became insupportable, and as we were going up a hill, and consequently proceeding rather slower than usual, I crept from the top of the coach and got snug into the basket.

As long as we went up hill, it was easy and pleasant. And, having had little or no sleep the night before, I was almost asleep among the trunks and the packages. But how was the case altered when we came to go down hill; then all the trunks and parcels began, as it were, to dance around me, and everything in the basket seemed to be alive, and I every moment received from them such violent blows that I thought my last hour was come.

I now write this as a warning to all strangers to stage coaches who may happen to take it into their heads, without being used to it, to take a place on the outside of an English post-coach; and still more, a place in the basket.'

Carl Moritz (1782)

12 May

Today is the birthday of Edward Lear (born in 1812), who wrote nonsense rhymes and comical poems that have delighted people, young and old, for more than 120 years. Here is one of them.

Once Mr Daddy Long-legs,
Dressed in brown and gray,
Walked about upon the sands
Upon a summer's day;
And there among the pebbles,
When the wind was rather cold,
He met with Mr Floppy Fly,
All dressed in blue and gold.
And as it was too soon to dine,
They drank some Periwinkle-wine,
And played an hour or two, or more,
At battlecock and shuttledore.

Said Mr Daddy Long-legs
To Mr Floppy Fly,
'Why do you never come to court?
I wish you'd tell me why.

All gold and shine, in dress so fine,
You'd quite delight the court.
Why do you never go at all?
I really think you *ought!*
And if you went, you'd see such sights!
Such rugs! and jugs! and candle-lights!
And more than all, the King and Queen,
One in red, and one in green!'

'O Mr Daddy Long-legs,'
Said Mr Floppy Fly,
'It's true I never go to court,
And I will tell you why.
If I had six long legs like yours,
At once I'd go to court!
But oh! I can't, because *my* legs
Are so extremely short.
And I'm afraid the King and Queen
(One in red, and one in green)
Would say aloud, 'You are not fit,
You Fly, to come to court a bit!'

'O Mr Daddy Long-legs,'
Said Mr Floppy Fly,
'I wish you'd sing one little song!
One mumbian melody!
You used to sing so awful well
In former days gone by,
But now you never sing at all;
I wish you'd tell me why:
For if you would, the silvery sound
Would please the shrimps and cockles round,
And all the crabs would gladly come
To hear you sing, 'Ah, Hum di Hum!'

Said Mr Daddy Long-legs,
'I can never sing again!
And if you wish, I'll tell you why,
Although it gives me pain.

For years I cannot hum a bit,
Or sing the smallest song;
And this the dreadful reason is,
My legs are grown too long!
My six long legs, all here and there,
Oppress my bosom with despair;
And if I stand, or lie, or sit,
I cannot sing one single bit!'

So Mr Daddy Long-legs
And Mr Floppy Fly
Sat down in silence by the sea,
And gazed upon the sky.
They said, 'This is a dreadful thing!
The world has all gone wrong,
Since one has legs too short by half,
The other much too long!
One never more can go to court,
Because his legs have grown too short;
The other cannot sing a song,
Because his legs have grown too long!'

Then Mr Daddy Long-legs
And Mr Floppy Fly
Rushed downward to the sea
With one sponge-taneous cry;
And there they found a little boat,
Whose sails were pink and gray;
And off they sailed among the waves,
Far, and far away.
They sailed across the silent main,
And reached the great Gromboolian plain;
And there they play for evermore
At battlecock and shuttledore.
The Daddy Long-legs and the Fly Edward Lear

12 **May**
Florence Nightingale was born in 1820.
See November 5th.

14 **May**
Nearly 200 years ago today (1796), a young boy named James Phipps helped in a very daring experiment. It probably saved his life. It certainly saved the lives of countless others who would otherwise have died in the following years.

This was the experiment. A doctor scratched James Phipps' arm. He took some liquid from a blister on a milkmaid's hand and put it in the scratch. Then everyone waited to see what would happen next.

The doctor, Edward Jenner, was trying to prevent the boy from catching the disease, smallpox. In those days, nearly everyone had it at some time in their lives, and out of every twelve victims, one would die. Many of those who survived went through their lives covered from head to foot with deep, ugly scars.

This was long before doctors knew anything about the causes of disease. They had no way of treating smallpox. But they *did* know that once someone had had it, they never caught it again.

Some doctors were trying to stop people getting the disease badly. They used a method which had been developed in Turkey. Fluid was taken from the blister of someone with mild smallpox, and put into a scratch on a child's arm. (This was called innoculation.) If it worked, the child would also get smallpox mildly, but then would never get the disease again. Sometimes, however, the child had more than a mild attack. Some even died. So this was not really a safe way of protecting anyone.

Dr Jenner had heard a tale which interested him. Country people said that if you got *cowpox*, you would never catch smallpox. Cowpox was a cattle disease, which milkmaids got from milking cows. They developed blisters rather like the smallpox ones but it was not such a serious disease.

Dr Jenner looked at every cowpox victim he

could find. He studied how the disease developed. He drew pictures of the spots at every stage.

Then James Phipps was brought to him. His mother was afraid he would get smallpox from their neighbour, and wanted the doctor to innoculate him. Jenner decided to do so, but using cowpox as an experiment.

The boy's arm came up in spots. But in just a few weeks they had completely healed. Two months later, it was time to try with smallpox. This was the real test. Would James catch the disease? If he did, would he get it very badly? Would he die? Would he be scarred for life?

James remained well. There was no sign of illness of any kind. The dose of cowpox had protected him, and Dr Jenner's daring experiment was a complete success.

Within a few years doctors all over Europe were following his method. In the one hundred years from 1700 to 1800, sixty million people had died in Europe from smallpox. Now it has been wiped off the earth, and people all over the world are being protected from many other diseases in much the same way as James Phipps was protected all those years ago.

14 **May**
Anniversary of founding of the State of Israel. ▶MCF.

The wheel around the world

1 If all the world's children
  Wanted to play holding hands,
  They could happily make
  A wheel around the sea. (Repeat)

2 If all the world's children
  Wanted to play holding hands,
  They could be sailors
  And build a bridge across the sea.
     (Repeat)

3 What a beautiful chorus we would make,
  Singing around the earth,
  If all the humans in the world
  Wanted to dance holding hands!

4 If all the world's children
  Wanted to play holding hands,
  They could happily make
  A wheel around the sea. (Repeat)

▶ECUS No 37

Traditional song from Mozambique
translated by Chris Searle
Music by Barrie Carson Turner

wheel a-round the sea. 2. If all the sea.

3. What a beau-ti-ful chor-us we would make, Sing-ing a-round the earth,

If all the hu-mans in the world_ Want-ed to dance hold-ing hands! If all the

CODA

sea. _____

Wesak

The festival of Wesak is taking place at the moment. It is a time when Buddhists celebrate important events in the life of the Buddha. This word means 'enlightened' or 'awakened' one – one who has become wise and learned to understand the world. It is the name people gave to an Indian prince named Siddartha Gautama who lived more than 2500 years ago, who chose a simple life of quiet meditation, searching out the meaning of sorrow and pain in the world, and learning how people could overcome it and be happy.

On Wesak, Buddhists celebrate his birth, his enlightenment, and his death. Here is the story of the night on which he became the 'enlightened one', the Buddha.

'Night fell and Siddartha still sat beneath the great tree.

In the darkness all around there were many rustlings and small movements and most people would have been greatly afraid in that place for it was as if all the powers of darkness and evil, all the thoughts of hate and despair had come to prevent Siddartha from ever being able to help men as he longed to help them. Mara, the Prince of Darkness and of all evil powers, brought with him all the horrid thoughts that live because of man's ignorance and cruelty and all the glooms and fears gathered around. Sometimes they appeared as shadows; they muttered like far off thunder and when lightning flickered they looked like horrid beasts lurking in the darkness. Everything seemed to be trying to keep Siddartha in his new-found strength from thinking any holy and peaceful thoughts.

Then there came to Siddartha the ten *great sins* to tempt him and to disturb his thoughts further. First came Attavanda, who always holds a mirror

May

so that she can see only her own face and she is one who thinks only about herself. She whispered to the Prince that he must seek for the great truth, the deep secret of Life, for himself, and then he would be the most powerful of gods. But Siddartha did not listen to her, knowing that he wanted the Truth for all men.

Then came Visikitcha who is also called Doubt and he whispered that Siddartha was trying to find out something which no one could ever find . . .

Then came False Faith, Sillabbat-paramasa, who defied any new hopes and said there were enough priests and temples already and no one wanted another religion. But Siddartha thought that he was seeking a Faith which would live more in men's hearts and minds than in any temples and church services.

Fourthly there came to him Passion, the King of the pleasure of love . . .

In the utter darkness then came six more terrible Sins, visions that were horrible and frightening. Fatigha or Hate came, wearing a girdle of serpents and as she cursed, the serpents hissed, but when Siddartha looked without fear there was silence again. Then came Ruparaga, who is greedy of time and snatches at each moment of pleasure as it passes, and Aruparaga, Fame, who tempts great heroes from self-love and the desire to be important, then Pride and Self Righteousness, Ignorance and Fear and Wrong. All these came up out of the darkness in a great storm. The earth shook and the heavens broke into drenching rain and everywhere the air was filled with horrid shapes and horrid sounds . . .

Dawn came at last and Siddartha, now to be called the Buddha, which means the Enlightened One, had come from the darkness into the light. Now he would pass among men not as a prince or a great king, but as one who carried with him a light of goodness and peace which would shed itself all around him, for he had come to a greater understanding of things than any man had ever come before. Now he would go back to the world of men and try to teach men to understand a little more of the purpose of living . . .

And the Buddha walked out from beneath his great tree and looked towards the rising sun and sang a great song, for the old life had gone for ever and a new life could now begin.'

The Bodhi Tree Greta James

20 May
Cricket Day in Italy. ▶ MCF.

23 May
Labour Day in Jamaica. ▶ MCF.

25 May
This day in 1935 has been called the greatest single day in the history of athletic achievement.

Jesse Owens, a young American athlete, set three new world records and equalled a fourth. His record for long jump 8.13m (26ft 8¼in) would last for 25 years.

He made history again the following year. At the 1936 Olympic games he won four gold medals. The games were taking place in front of Adolf Hitler, the Nazi dictator of Germany. At the time he was saying that the Germanic white race was better in every way than any other race. The Olympic games were meant to help prove this to everyone present, and, more importantly, to the rest of the world.

Jesse Owens was black. His tremendous achievements surpassed those of any other athlete at the Games. There could be no better proof that Hitler's ideas were nonsense.

Hitler was so angry that he walked out of the stadium, refusing to congratulate Jesse at the ceremonies to present the medals. But at these same Olympics there was a gesture of great sporting generosity to Jesse from a rival. The main threat to his winning had been the German athlete, Luz Long. During the qualifying long jump final, Jesse twice overstepped the take-off board and made 'no jumps'. He had only one more chance to qualify. Now, his arch rival Luz Long suggested that he take a longer run up.

Jesse followed his advice, jumped successfully, qualified for the final, and went on to win the gold medal, setting a new Olympic record in the process.

It was not surprising that Americans in their thousands flocked to the streets to welcome him on his return. He was applauded for his double success – as an athlete, and as a human being defying the stupidity of Hitler's vicious ideas.

The man and the lion

A man and a lion were travelling together, and as they journeyed on their way, each boasted about himself, saying that he was stronger and more brave than his companion, each claiming a greater power.

The argument raged on, until at last they reached a crossroads. There they found themselves before a statue of a man strangling a lion.

'See,' the man said with pride. 'That proves what I've been saying. The statue shows that we are far more powerful than you.'

'I wouldn't say so,' replied the lion. 'That is just how *you* see it. If lions created statues, you can be sure that most of them would show the man at the worst end of the struggle!'

There are two sides to every question.

Adapted from Aesop

28 May

On this day in 1860, there were such violent storms around the coast of Britain, that 143 ships were wrecked. What would a violent storm at sea have been like in a sailing ship over 120 years ago? Here is one account:

'In two days it blew a gale. The *Judea*, hove to, wallowed on the Atlantic like an old candle-box. It blew day after day: it blew with spite, without interval, without mercy, without rest. The world was nothing but an immensity of great foaming waves rushing at us, under a sky low enough to touch with the hand and dirty like a smoked ceiling. In the stormy space surrounding us there was as much flying spray as air. Day after day and night after night there was nothing round the ship but the howl of the wind, the tumult of the sea, the noise of water pouring over her deck. There was no rest for her and no rest for us. She tossed, she pitched, she stood on her head, she sat on her tail, she rolled, she groaned, and we had to hold on while on deck and cling to our bunks when below, in a constant effort of body and worry of mind.

We pumped all the four hours. We pumped all night, all day, all the week – watch and watch. She was working herself loose, and leaked badly – not enough to drown us at once, but enough to kill us with the work at the pumps. And while we pumped the ship was going from us piecemeal: the bulwarks went, the stanchions were torn out, the ventilators smashed, the cabin-door burst in. There was not a dry spot in the ship. She was being gutted bit by bit. The long-boat changed, as if by magic, into matchwood where she stood in her gripes. I had lashed her myself, and was rather proud of my handiwork, which had withstood so long the malice of the sea. And we pumped. And there was no break in the weather. The sea was white like a sheet of foam, like a cauldron of boiling milk; there was not a break in the clouds, no – not the size of a man's hand – no, not for so much as ten seconds. There was for us no sky, there were for us no stars, no sun, no universe – nothing but angry clouds and an infuriated sea. We pumped watch and watch, for dear life; and it seemed to last for months, for years, for all eternity, as though we had been dead and gone to a hell for sailors. We forgot the day of the week, the name of the month, what year it was, and whether we had ever been ashore. The sails blew away, she lay broadside on under a weather-cloth, the ocean poured over her, and we did not care. We turned those handles, and had the eyes of idiots. As soon as we had crawled on deck I used to take a round turn with a rope about the men, the pumps, and the main mast, and we turned, we turned incessantly, with the water to our waists, to our necks, over our heads. It was all one. We had forgotten how it felt to be dry.'

Youth Joseph Conrad

This was before many of the safety measures which make ships so much safer nowadays. (*See* February 10th, April 14–15th.)

May

29 May

'We stepped up. We were there. The dream had come true . . .' So wrote one of the two men who first reached the top of Mt Everest, the highest mountain in the world.

Rising 8848m high among the Himalaya Mountains on the 'roof of the world', it is called Chomolungma, Goddess Mother of the World, by local people. For over thirty years, expedition after expedition had tried to reach the summit. Seven in all had made the attempt. Seven had failed. Some ended in death for the climbers.

Then in 1953, an expedition led by Colonel John Hunt made their attempt. On May 29th, two men reached the summit.

They were Edmund Hillary, a New Zealander, and Tenzing Norgay, a Sherpa – one of the mountain people who live in the shadow of Mount Everest. Born and bred among these peaks and valleys, they are tough and knowledgeable, and many act as guides on climbing expeditions.

Here, in Tenzing Norgay's own words, is what happened:

'Many times I think of that morning at Camp Nine. We have spent the night there, Hillary and I, in our little tent at almost 28,000 feet (8540m), which is the highest that men have ever slept. It has been a cold night. Hillary's boots are frozen, and we are almost frozen too. But now in the grey light, when we creep from the tent, there is almost no wind. The sky is clear and still. And that is good.

We look up. For weeks, for months, that is all we have done. Look up. And there it is – the top of Everest. Only it is different now – so near, so close, only a little more than a thousand feet, above us. It is no longer just a dream, a high dream in the sky, but a real and solid thing, a thing of rock and snow, that men can climb. We make ready. We will climb it. This time, with God's help, we will climb on to the end.

Then I look down. All the rest of the world is under us. To the west Nuptse; to the south Lhotse; to the east Makalu: all of them great mountain-tops, and beyond them hundreds of others, all under us. Straight down the ridge, two thousand feet down, is the South Col, where our nearest friends wait – Sahibs Lowe and Gregory and the young Sherpa Ang Nyima, who yesterday helped us up to Camp Nine. Below that is the white wall of Lhotse, four thousand feet more, and at its bottom the Western Cwm, where the rest of our friends wait at the advance base camp. Below the Cwm is the Icefall, below the Icefall the Khumbu Glacier. I see that Hillary is looking too, and I point. Below the glacier, 16,000 feet (4880m) down, you can just see in the grey light the old monastery of Thyangboche.

To Hillary, perhaps, it does not mean much. To a man from the West it is only a far, strange place in a far, strange country. But for me it is home. Beyond Thyangboche are the valleys and villages of Solo Khumbu, and there I was born and grew up. On the tall hillsides above them I climbed as a boy, tending my father's yaks. Home is close now. I can almost stretch out my hand and touch it. But if it is close it is also far. Much farther than 16,000 feet (4880m). As we strap on our oxygen-tanks I think back to the boy, so close and so far, who had never heard of oxygen, but yet looked up at this mountain and dreamed.

Then we turn round, Hillary and I. We begin to climb. It is many miles and many years that have brought me here . . .

On top of the rock-cliff we rest again. Certainly after the climb up the gap, we are both a bit breathless, but after some slow pulls at the oxygen I am feeling fine. I look up; the top is very close now; and my heart thumps with excitement and joy. Then we are on our way again . . . About thirty feet away we stop for a minute and look up. Then we go on . . .

We stepped up. We were there. The dream had come true . . .

What we did first was what all climbers do when they reach the top of their mountain. We shook hands. But this was not enough for Everest. I waved my arms in the air, and then threw them round Hillary, and we thumped each other on the back until, even with the oxygen, we were almost breathless. Then we looked round. It was eleven-thirty in the morning, the sun was shining, and the sky was the deepest blue I have ever seen.'

Man of Everest James Ramsey Ullman

In some years the following festivals may occur in June:

Martyrdom of Guru Arjan Dev Sikh festival. ▶F&F.

Ramadan. ▶MCF. **Night of Power** (see below) also ▶F&F. **Eid-ul-Fitr.** ▶F&F.

Rogationtide. ▶MCF.

Wesak Buddhist festival. *See* May page 89. ▶F&F

Whitsun (Pentecost). ▶F&F.

June's name

The month of June gets its name from Juno, Roman goddess of heavenly light, goddess of the moon. She was seen as the protector and defender of women throughout their lives, and particularly during childbirth. She also watched over marriages – so the tradition in this country that June is a good month for weddings comes from these ancient beliefs about Juno.

She was also mother of Mars, god of war, and one of her main festivals was celebrated in March, the month named after Mars. It was a family festival in which the wives and mothers of Roman households were the central figures, and were given presents.

There is a story that when Rome was attacked by enemies, it was Juno's sacred animals, the geese, who warned the Romans of their danger. After this, Juno was also seen as adviser to the Romans.

The night of power

On the 27th day of Ramadan, Muslims celebrate a festival called Lailat ul-Qadr, the Night of Power, and tell the story of how Muhammad was called to the service of God. This is that story.

Muhammad was weary of his life as a merchant.

It felt empty. He was bored and yearned for something more to give him purpose in his life.

To escape his discontent he had begun to wander up into the mountains to spend time there in the tranquil air, among the gentle sheep.

One night, he had been sitting in his usual place, lost for many hours in quiet thought and prayer. Suddenly a voice broke the stillness, seeming to come from deep within himself, and yet from all the corners of the cave, and even from the mountain slopes outside, echoing in the valleys and along the peaks, filling the night with sound.

As he stared around, an angel appeared, holding a cloth of green brocade before Muhammad's eyes. On the cloth were words he could not understand.

'Read,' the angel said.

Muhammad was puzzled. 'What shall I read?' For answer, the angel clasped him firmly, then let him go again.

'Read', he was told.

'What shall I read?'

Again the angel held him. The grip was firm and strong and could not be escaped . . .

'Read', for the third time the voice rang out.

'Read'. *In the name of thy Lord who created man from a drop of blood: read in the name of Almighty God who taught man the use of the pen and taught him what he knew not before . . .*

As each word issued from the angel's mouth, Muhammad caught it and whispered it until it felt as though every letter was carved deep within his heart and mind and he knew that they would never leave him, ever again.

Then he was alone again. The angel had gone. Panic flooded through him, confusing his mind. What was it that had happened to him here? Was he going mad? Had he seen ghosts?

He rose, and moved out of the cave into the night.

And then there came the voice again:

'*Oh Muhammad! Truly thou art the messenger of God and I am his angel, Gabriel.*'

He looked up, and there he saw the angel, gigantic, filling the night with light, straddling the earth. And every way he turned, he was still there, so that there was no escape from him.

Then he was gone, and it was dark.

Dawn came. Muhammad turned, and began his journey down the mountain path to home.

And so began a time when he received many visits from the angel Gabriel. On each, he heard the angel's words, spoke them aloud and told them to his followers. In turn they wrote them down on scraps of leather, bits of pottery, palm leaves. Later they were collected, and became the book, the Qur'an, which is the Muslim holy scriptures.

Dragon Boat Festival

This Chinese festival falls in June. ▶F&F.

Joy in summer

There is joy in
Feeling the warmth
Come into the great world
And seeing the sun
Follow its old footprints
Into the summer night.

There is fear in
Feeling the cold
Come into the great world
And seeing the moon
– New new moon, now full moon –
Follow its old footprints
In the winter night.

Eskimo Chant, translated by Knud Rasmussen

See also song on pages 94 and 101.

Winds in summer

Tradional Bohemian
arr. Gordon Hitchcock

1   Winds in summer softly blow
    O'er the fields of corn that grow,
    Blossoms tumble from the trees
    With each gentle breeze.

2   When the sun shines bright and warm,
    All the fields are then so calm.
    And upon the distant hill,
    All the woods are still.

1. Winds in sum-mer soft-ly blow

O'er the fields of corn that grow,   Blos-soms tum-ble from the trees   With each gen-tle breeze.

Chime bars 1

Chime bars 2

10 June

Imagine a machine made like this: a large, heavy, curved wooden frame; a horse's head carved on the front; two enormous iron-tyred wheels; pedals worked by pushing the feet continually backwards and forwards.

This is a description of the first bicycle ever built. It was made by a Scottish blacksmith named Kirkpatrick Macmillan over 140 years ago in 1839. He simply wanted to travel around the countryside, for work, faster than he could walk or ride a horse. So he invented a machine to do so!

You can imagine that he caused quite a commotion at first – particularly when, a few years later, he decided to ride 40 miles into Glasgow. There was such a crush and push of curious spectators to see his 'wood and iron horse' as he entered the city, that he knocked a child down. So Kirkpatrick was unfortunate enough to also commit the first cycling offence.

It was actually in France, some 20 years later, that people started making bicycles for sale to the general public, and they were brought from France to Britain. Within a few years, the newspapers were talking of a 'new terror' in the streets, for the speed with which these vehicles swept along the roads, compared with horsedrawn traffic, amazed everyone, and frightened quite a few.

See also July page 102.

11 June

On this day about 90 years ago (1895), a new kind of competition took place. It was a race of 'horseless carriages' – the first ever motor-race. The winner drove at an average of 24km (15 miles) per hour, a most impressive speed at the time! It took him 48 hours to drive the course from Paris to Bordeaux in France, and back again – a round trip of 1178km (732 miles).

23 cars started out. Only eight petrol-driven vehicles and one steamcar actually arrived back. Nevertheless the spectators and the drivers thought the race was a great success and it was not long before others were held – from Paris to Vienna, in Austria, and from Paris to Berlin, in Germany.

These early races were all quite dangerous events. The motor cars rattled along on rutted roads, steering wildly round dogs and farm carts which appeared unexpectedly on the road in front. When trying to pass another car, the driver simply had to guess the position of both car and road, by the tops of trees which rose above the clouds of dust.

And if they weren't thick with dust, the roads were likely, just as quickly, to become quagmires of mud at the first sign of rain.

However, the new kind of event rapidly became very popular, for people were fascinated by the new machines, and manufacturers were able to test the cars in public, and so produce better and better designs.

It was not long before the first regular international races began. One of them was the French Grand Prix (begun in 1906), which continues to this day.

12 June

Independent Republic Day in the Philippines. ▶MCF.

Fire! Fire!

At this time of year, you often see warnings about the danger of fires in country areas. They are easy to ignore – to think of as not very important, because we think of course *we'll* be very careful and *we* wouldn't be so stupid as to start a fire which we couldn't put out.

Here is a story about a forest fire in Australia. It is about three boys who set off into the hills for a week of camping. When passers-by tell them not to make a fire, they treat this instruction as just another boring piece of nagging.

During the night, the boys wake in their tent, thirsty and hot. They try to light a small stove which runs on methylated spirits, hoping to make themselves a drink . . .

'The battery's flat. Blooming thing. Must have been a crook battery. Hardly used it at all. *Now* look what I've done! There's the metho bottle knocked for six.'

'You dope,' cried Wallace. 'Pick it up quick. Or we'll lose it all.'

'The cork's in it.' Graham groped for it . . . and said, 'Crumbs.'

'Now what?'

'The cork's *not* in it, that's what. It must have come out.'

'How could it come out? Honest to goodness –'

'It's *burning*,' howled Graham.

A blue flame snaked from the little heater up through the rocks towards the bottle in the boy's hand; or at least that was how it seemed to happen. It happened so swiftly it may have deceived the eye. Instinctively, to protect himself,

June

Graham threw the bottle away. There was a shower of fire from its neck, as from the nozzle of a hose.

'Oh my gosh,' yelled Wallace and tore off his sleeping bag. 'Harry!' he screamed. 'Wake up, Harry!'

They tried to stamp on the fire, but their feet were bare and they couldn't find their shoes. They tried to smother it with their sleeping-bags, but *it* seemed to be everywhere. Harry couldn't even escape from his bag; he couldn't find the zip fastener, and for a few awful moments in his confusion between sleep and wakefulness he thought he was in his bed at home and the house had burst into flames around him. He couldn't come to grips with the situation; he knew only dismay and the wildest kind of alarm. Graham and Wallace, panicking, were throwing themselves from place to place, almost sobbing, beating futilely at a widening arc of fire. Every desperate blow they made seemed to fan the fire, to scatter it farther, to feed it.

'Put it out,' shouted Graham. 'Put it out.'

It wasn't dark any longer. It was a flickering world of tree trunks and twisted boughs, of scrub and saplings and stones, of shouts and wind and smoke and frantic fear. It was so quick. It was terrible.

'Put it out,' cried Graham, and Harry fought out of his sleeping-bag, knowing somehow that they'd never get it out by beating at it, that they'd have to get water up from the creek. But all they had was a four-pint billy can.

The fire was getting away from them in all directions, crackling through the scrub downwind, burning fiercely back into the wind. Even the ground was burning; grass, roots, and fallen leaves were burning, humus was burning. There were flames on the trees, bark was burning, foliage was flaring, flaring like a whip-crack; and the heat was savage and searing and awful to breathe.

'We can't, we can't,' cried Wallace. 'What are we going to do?'

They beat at it and beat at it and beat at it.

'Oh gee,' sobbed Graham. He was crying, and he hadn't cried since he was twelve years old. 'What have I done? *We've got to get it out!*' ...

'For Pete's sake run!' shouted Harry.

Something in his voice seemed to get through to Wallace and Graham and they ran, the three of them, like frightened rabbits. They ran this way and that, hugging their packs and their scorched sleeping-bags, blundering into the scrub, even into the trunks of trees. Fire and confusion seemed to be all around them. The fire's rays darted through the bush; it was an endless chain with a will of its own, encircling and entangling them, or like a wall that leapt out of the earth to block every fresh run they made for safety. Even the creek couldn't help them. They didn't know where it was. There might as well not have been a creek at all.

'This way,' shouted Harry. 'A track.'

They stumbled back down the track towards Tinley; at least they thought it was towards Tinley, they didn't really know. Perhaps they were running to save their lives, running simply from fear, running away from what they had done.

When they thought they were safe they hid close to a partly constructed house. They could hear sirens wailing; lights were coming on here and there; the head lamps of cars were beaming and sweeping around curves in the track. They could hear shouts on the wind, they heard a woman cry hysterically, they heard Graham sobbing.

Over all was a red glow.'

Ash Road, Ivan Southall

This story reminds us that, particularly in hot weather when everything is very dry, fires are started very easily and quickly get out of control. We must never forget this and be very careful at all times. Even an empty bottle or piece of glass can start a fire.

See also Class Assembly page 119.

15 June

In 1942, two girls, their parents, and four other people went into secret rooms in a building in Amsterdam, and sealed themselves in. If they had not done so, they would have ended up in concentration camps, along with hundreds of other people from the streets around them. For this was the second world war; the Nazis had invaded Holland, and all Jews were being rounded up and taken away.

They stayed in hiding for two years. We know all about this time, because one of the girls, Anne Frank, wrote a diary. She tells the day-to-day story of this strange existence, cut off completely from the outer world. Each day brings greater fear of discovery. But Anne refuses to despair, and succeeds always in believing that everything evil in the world will, in the end, be overcome.

At one time, she wrote.

'And as for us, we are fortunate. Yes, we are luckier than millions of people. It is quiet and safe here. We are even so selfish as to talk about 'after the war,' brighten up at the thoughts of having new clothes and new shoes, whereas we really ought to save every penny, to help other people, and save what is left from the wreckage after the war.'

But the family were betrayed and sent to concentration camps. This is what Anne wrote on June 15th, 1944, less than two months before their hiding place was found:

'I wonder if it's because I haven't been able to poke my nose outdoors for so long that I've grown so crazy about everything to do with nature? I can perfectly well remember that there was a time when a deep blue sky, the song of the birds, moonlight and flowers would have never kept me spellbound. That's changed since I've been here.

At Whitsun, for instance, when it was ever so warm, I stayed awake on purpose until half-past eleven one evening in order to have a good look at the moon for once by myself. Alas, the sacrifice was all in vain, as the moon gave far too much light and I didn't dare risk opening a window. Another time, some months ago now, I happened to be upstairs one evening when the window was open. I didn't go downstairs until the window had to be shut. The dark, rainy evening, the gale, the scudding clouds held me entirely in their power; it was the first time in a year and a half that I'd seen the night face to face. After that evening my longing to see it again was greater than my fear of burglars, rats, and raids on the house. I went downstairs all by myself and looked outside through the windows in the kitchen and the private office. A lot of people are fond of nature, many sleep outdoors occasionally, and people in prisons and hospitals long for the day when they will be free to enjoy the beauties of nature, but few are so shut away and isolated from that which can be shared alike by rich and poor. It's not imagination on my part when I say that to look up at the sky, the clouds, the moon and the stars makes me calm and patient . . . Mother Nature makes me humble and prepared to face every blow courageously.

Alas, it has had to be that I am only able – except on a few rare occasions – to look at nature through dirty net curtains hanging before very dusty windows . . .'

Diary of Anne Frank

They all died in the concentration camps, except for Anne's father. Anne herself died three months before she would have turned sixteen. But her diary remains with us, a story of people's courage in times of great sorrow and hardship, and a reminder to us all that such things should not be allowed to happen again.

17 June

Children's Day in Indonesia. ▶MCF.

Early days at Wimbledon

Imagine playing tennis in a long white dress with billowing skirts, thick black stockings, black shoes, and a white straw hat. This is how women dressed to play when the first women's championship took place at Wimbledon a hundred years ago.

The men's fashions seem equally strange now. White flannel shirts, complete with tie, were worn; long white trousers hoisted up with a belt, and a white cap.

Even the rackets were different, square at the top, and the ball was much lighter than the one used nowadays.

Wimbledon began in 1877. A few years earlier, the All-England Croquet Club had begun to allow tennis to be played on one of its lawns. In 1877 they decided to hold a championship for amateur players (players who were not earning any money from tennis).

22 people entered that very first competition. It was rather different from the Wimbledon of today. There were only 200 spectators, and no stand for them to sit in. They each paid a shilling to watch the final. After the match, the nets, posts and guy ropes were sold at a price of 30 shillings for the set, and the club made a profit of £10 on the event!

That year the men's champion was Spencer W

Gore. When the first women's championship took place seven years later, Maud Watson won it two years running.

Prizes also used to be rather different from nowadays. One of the winners in the 1920s was presented with a £5 voucher to a London jewellery shop!

Father's Day

In North America, Britain and Commonwealth countries, Father's Day is celebrated on the third Sunday in June. ▶MCF.

June

A prayer for rain

Times of drought, when no rain falls for months, sometimes years, on end, can bring terrible famine to a people.

Without rain, no crops can grow – their grain, their vegetables, their fruit – all wither and die. The livestock – cattle and goats, pigs and sheep – will also die of thirst. Without the crops and animals, there is no food for people, now or in the future.

And people themselves cannot live without water, either. It is their lifeline, too.

This is a Rain Song, a prayer for rain, from the Pima Indians of North America. The down and feathers of the eagle are the rain clouds gathering in the sky.

Hi-iya, naiho-o! The earth is rumbling
From the beating of our basket drums.
The earth is rumbling from the beating
Of our basket drums, everywhere humming.
Earth is rumbling, everywhere raining.

Hi-iya, naiho-o! Pluck out the feathers
From the wing of the eagle and turn them
Toward the east where lie the large clouds.
Hi-iya, naiho-o! Pluck out the soft down
From the breast of the eagle and turn it
Toward the west where sail the small clouds.
Hi-iya, naiho-o! Beneath the abode
Of the rain gods it is thundering;
Large corn is there. *Hi-iya, naiho-o!*
Beneath the abode of the rain gods
It is raining; small corn is there.

Rain Song Pima Indians

21 June

Midsummer in the northern hemisphere; midwinter in the southern. ▶MCF.

The electric kite

More than 230 years ago (1752) a man went out into a raging thunderstorm to fly a kite. A strange thing to do, you probably think. The man was Benjamin Franklin, and he was conducting an experiment. We know now that the experiment was very dangerous and might easily have killed him.

He survived, and the results of his experiment were very important. He wanted to find out if lightning was electricity. At that time not much was known about electricity. There were a few machines which could make tiny sparks. But it was a long time before the electric motor or any kind of battery was invented. People played with the small electricity machines for fun. It was interesting to see the sparks created, or to feel a tiny electric shock. They had no understanding of what they were using, either of its possible power, or the danger in it. But Benjamin Franklin was both a practical man and a great thinker. He was interested in finding out what *use* this fascinating force might have.

He knew that metal attracts electricity. If he could find a way of drawing the lightning downwards, attract it with something metal, then perhaps he could collect the lightning and prove it really was electricity.

So he flew his kite. It was covered with silk, and had a metal rod attached to it. He hoped the lightning would run down the rod, the kite, the wet string attached to the kite, and into the metal key which he tied to the bottom of the string. Within minutes of raising his kite into the storm, the string began to bristle and Franklin felt the prickle of an electric current in the key!

It wasn't long before he had worked out a way of using this new knowledge. If he fixed a piece of metal to the side of a tall building, higher than the building, and ran it down the side, into the earth below, surely the lightning would run down this metal, into the earth, leaving the building quite unharmed?

And so the lightning conductor was born. At first it led to all kinds of weird and wonderful ideas. One man in France invented a portable lightning conductor which fitted into his umbrella!

Franklin's way of protecting buildings from being hit by lightning is still being used today. When he first tried it out, it was the first time that knowledge of electricity was put to any practical use. Nowadays, most of our way of life in this country depends on electricity. So, in a way, we have the far-sighted Benjamin Franklin to thank for that.

24 June

Midsummer Day festival and the Christian feast day of Saint John the Baptist. ▶MCF.

Monsoon danger

Through the summer, monsoon clouds gather over India. They bring much-needed rain, to water the crops and satisfy the animals' thirst. But they bring dangers too . . .

Here is the story about a young girl who lives on a tiny island in the middle of a river. As the rain falls day after day, she sees the river rising around her and climbs to the highest place she can find – the spreading branches of an ancient tree . . .

'The water was rising rapidly now, and all that remained of the island was the big rock that supported the hut, and the top of the hut itself, and the peepul tree.

It was a tall tree, with many branches, and it seemed unlikely that the water could ever go right over it. But how long would Sita have to remain there? . . .

Other things came floating out of the hut – a large pumpkin; a red turban belonging to Grandfather, unwinding in the water like a long snake; and then – Mumta!

The doll, being filled with straw and wood-shavings, moved quite swiftly on the water and passed close to the peepul tree. Sita saw it, and wanted to call out, to urge her friend to make for the tree; but she knew that Mumta could not swim – the doll could only float, travel with the river, and perhaps be washed ashore many miles downstream . . .

The river swirled all around her now. It was almost up to the roof of the hut. Soon the mud walls would crumble and vanish. Except for the big rock, and some trees far, far away, there was only water to be seen.

For a moment or two Sita glimpsed a boat with several people in it moving sluggishly away from the ruins of a flooded village, and she thought she saw someone pointing towards her; but the river swept them on, and the boat was lost to view.

The river was very angry, it was like a wild beast, a dragon on the rampage, thundering down from the hills and sweeping across the plain, bringing with it dead animals, uprooted trees, household goods, and huge fish choked to death by the swirling mud.

The tall old peepul tree groaned. Its long, winding roots clung tenaciously to the earth from which the tree had sprung many, many years ago. But the earth was softening, the stones were being washed away. The roots of the tree were rapidly losing their hold . . .

The tree groaned and moved again. It had seen many monsoons. Once before, it had stood firm while the river had swirled around its massive trunk. But it had been young then.

Now, old in years and tired of standing still, the tree was ready to join the river.

With a flurry of its beautiful leaves, and a surge of mud from below, the tree left its place in the earth, and, tilting, moved slowly forward, turning a little from side to side, dragging its roots along the ground. To Sita it seemed as though the river was rising to meet the sky. Then the tree moved into the main current of the river, and went a little faster, swinging Sita from side to side. Her feet were in the water but she clung tenaciously to her branch.

The branches swayed, but Sita did not lose her grip. The water was very close now. Sita was frightened. She could not see the extent of the flood or the width of the river. She could only see the immediate danger, the water surrounding the tree . . .

Sita felt very tired. Her arms were aching, and she was no longer upright. With the tree almost on its side, she had to cling tightly to her branch to avoid falling off. The grey weeping sky was like a great shifting dome.

She knew she could not remain much longer in that position. It might be better to try swimming to some distant rooftop or tree. Then she heard someone calling. Craning her neck to look upriver, she was able to make out a small boat coming directly towards her.

The boat approached the tree. There was a boy in the boat who held on to one of the branches to steady himself, giving his free hand to Sita.

She grasped it, and slipped into the boat beside him.

The boy placed his bare foot against the tree-trunk and pushed away.

The little boat moved swiftly down the river. The big tree was left far behind. Sita would never see it again.

Angry River Ruskin Bond

Eventually Sita and her rescuer reached a village. There, people took them in, offering food and shelter till the floods went down.

In time, the waters began to fall a little lower. People began to repair their homes and fields. Sita left her friends and set off to find her own family again. She survived. For even in the most terrifying times, people are generous to one another, and help each other to pick up the pieces and start life anew after any disaster.

See also April page 80.

July

Dhammacakka, the Buddhist festival, occurs in July. ▶F&F.

July's name

This month is named after Julius Caesar, the Roman Emperor. It was once called simply 'the fifth month', for at the time the Romans began their year not in January, but in the spring – in March.

About 2030 years ago, Julius Caesar made important changes to the calendar. The year became 365 days long. The calendar months became twelve roughly equal periods of time, and were no longer measured by the moon. Lastly, Julius Caesar changed the beginning of the year to January.

As the fifth month was his birth month, it was named Julius in his honour – from which we get July.

It is this calendar, begun 2030 years ago, which is the basis of the one that we use officially in this country now. Of course, for festivals and religious events, many people measure the months by the waxing and waning of the moon.

The Indians of North America give names to their months, which tell vividly of the passing seasons of the year. The moon month which usually begins at the end of July is called:

The moon when the deer horns drop off. (Kiowa Indians)

The little ripening moon (followed, a month later, by The Big- ripening moon). (Creek Indians)

Moon when the wild cherries are ripe. (Sioux Indians)

The moon when the corn pops. (Winnebago Indians)

If we used names like this, how would you name this month?
See also January page 49, February 29th, March page 70.

1 July

Dominion Day in Canada. ▶MCF.

History in nursery rhymes

July was one of the worst months in the Great Plague 320 years ago. At one time, in 1665, 6000 people were dying each week, infected by the plague-carrying fleas on the rats which infested towns and cities.

This may all seem a long time ago. But you may know the rhyme:

> 'Ring-a-ring o' roses,
> A pocket full of posies.
> Atishoo, Atishoo,
> We all fall down!'

The rhyme is usually chanted to accompany a group of children holding hands in a ring, dancing round, then falling in a heap, (with lots of giggles) at the last line.

Actually, the rhyme is telling of the gruesome progress of the deadly plague, and is a very old song. Some people think it is even older than the Great Plague, and refers to the Black Death 630 years ago, which was a different kind of plague.

Whichever epidemic the song refers to, the meaning is the same: The 'ring-a-ring o' roses' is the mark which appeared on the skin of victims of the disease. The 'pocket full of posies' are the herbs which people carried to try (in vain) to protect themselves from it – pouches of nutmeg, rue, cloves, cinnamon, elder leaves and onions.

One of the earliest signs of the plague was a lot of sneezing – hence 'Atishoo, Atishoo;' and, of course, 'We all fall down' is the likely end of the disease – collapse and death.

There are many other rhymes which tell of events in history. There's 'London Bridge is falling down' (about all the unsuccessful ideas to repair the old London Bridge) and 'London's burning' which tells of the great fire (*see* 2nd–6th September).

There is another, which you probably would not think had any special meaning.

> 'Baa, baa black sheep, have you any wool?
> Yes sir, yes sir, three bags full.
> One for the master, and one for the dame.
> And one for the little boy (girl)
> Who lives down the lane.'

This little song is about the miserable lives of farming workers 400 to 500 years ago. At the time, merchants were making a great deal of money buying and selling wool. A lot of land which had been used for growing crops was now turned over to sheep grazing. It had needed many labourers to farm crops on the land. It needed only one shepherd to tend quite a large herd of sheep.

So there were many labourers without work. The wool merchants grew richer and richer, gathering wool and sending it to London to exchange for luxuries – silks, jewels, spices – from other countries. Farming workers and their families, with no way of earning any money, starved.

Some people now think that 'One for the master' is talking about the king; 'one for the dame' is about the wool merchants; and 'one for the little boy or little girl down the lane' are all the poor people who only ever got a paltry third of everything they worked to produce.

Summer
is a happy time

1   Holidays are nearly here now,
    We are planning what to do,
    Swimming, cycling, going camping,
    Trips to France so parlez vous!

2   Early mornings cool and lovely,
    Then the sun grows hot and strong,
    Beating down on drowsy noondays,
    Summer evenings warm and long.

3   Summer is a happy time and
    Sunshine leaves us feeling good;
    We can spread that happiness by
    Helping others as we should.

    Second part all verses:
    Listen now and sing together
    Make the most of summer weather.

▶ ECUS No 2

T. Goodban (1784 — 1863)
Words and arrangement by Mark S. Johnson

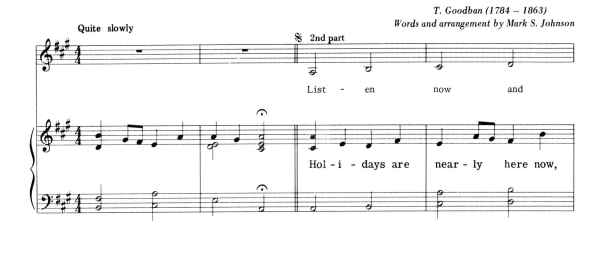

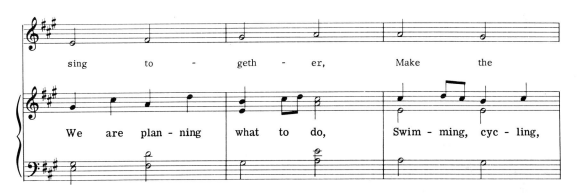

July

4 July
Independence Day in the USA. ▶MCF

Man the harvester

Traditional stories often tell a lot about people's way of life. This story is told by farming people who live in the Sudan in Africa, near that part of the River Nile called the White Nile. It shows how closely they are bound to the cultivation of the land, and the growing of their grain crop, millet.

The Creator made the earth. Now he wandered, admiring it.

How beautiful it looked! Birds sang. Insects buzzed and fluttered. Trees and grass and plants grew green. In the rivers, waters glistened.

It was almost complete. But not quite, he thought. It needs a creature who can till the soil and reap its riches.

He pondered this. What shape should the creature be? It must be able to move – to walk and jump and run, to leave its home and go into the fields to work the soil. Then, in the distance, the Creator saw a shimmering lake, pink-rimmed with flamingoes wading on their long and elegant legs. Legs, thought the Creator, the new creature must have legs, like the flamingo. Long, slender, powerful legs.

It must be able to plant and sow the seed, to pull the weeds and reap the harvest when the crops are ripe. It must have hands to grasp the hoe and swing the scythe. It must have arms, the Creator thought.

And it has to see the millet growing, to care for it through all its seasons. It must have eyes for this.

And a mouth, to eat the crop. A tongue, to speak, to dance, to shout. For, the Creator asked himself, will the creature not need celebration when the work is done?

And if it has a tongue, then it must have two ears, to hear the dance and music and the speech of others. This way it can be wise and learn all there is to know.

So the Creator began his work. He travelled on. Everywhere were lands of different soils. Rich, moist soils around the rivers and lakes. Soft, powdery sand bleached by the sea along its shores. Black soils, red soils, white soils, yellow soils . . .

He marvelled at the variety he found. He took some of each, and mixed it to a clay. Then he began to knead, moulding it to the shape he'd planned.

And from each different clay he made a different coloured person – yellow, black, brown, white . . .

Then he sat back and looked. How pleased he was with them! They stood before him, each one perfect, each one eager to be sent into the world to begin their work.

And so he sent them.

See also Class Assembly page 120.

Early days of bicycles

This is what a country district in Britain was like about 100 years ago:

'Apart from the occasional carriages and the carrier's cart twice a week, there was little traffic on that road beyond the baker's van and the farm carts and wagons. Sometimes a woman from a neighbouring village or hamlet would pass through on foot, shopping basket on arm, on her way to the market town. It was thought nothing of then to walk six or seven miles to purchase a reel of cotton or a packet of tea, or sixpen'orth of pieces from the butcher to make a meat pudding for Sunday. Excepting the carrier's cart, which only came on certain days, there was no other way of travelling. It was thought quite dashing to ride with Old Jimmy, but frightfully extravagant, for the fare was sixpence. Most people preferred to go on foot and keep the sixpence to spend when they got there.

But although it was not yet realized, the revolution in transport had begun. The first high 'penny-farthing' bicycles were already on the roads, darting and swerving like swallows heralding the summer of the buses and cars and motor cycles which were soon to transform country life. But how fast those new bicycles travelled and how dangerous they looked! Pedestrians backed almost into the hedges when they met one of them, for was there

not almost every week in the Sunday newspapers the story of someone being knocked down and killed by a bicycle, and letters from readers saying cyclists ought not to be allowed to use the roads which, as everybody knew, were provided for people to walk on or to drive on behind horses. 'Bicyclists ought to have roads to themselves, like railway trains' was the general opinion.

Yet it was thrilling to see a man hurtling through space on one high wheel, with another tiny wheel wobbling hopelessly behind. You wondered how they managed to keep their balance. No wonder they wore an anxious air . . .

Cycling was looked upon as a passing craze and the cyclists in their tight navy knickerbocker suits and pillbox caps with the badge of their club in front were regarded as figures of fun. None of those in the hamlet who rushed out to their gates to see one pass, half hoping for and half fearing a spill, would have believed, if they had been told, that in a few years there would be at least one bicycle in every one of their houses, that the men would ride to work on them and the younger women, when their housework was done, would lightly mount 'the old bike' and pedal away to the market town to see the shops. They would have been still more incredulous had they been told that many of them would live to see every child of school age in the hamlet provided by a kind County Council with a bicycle on which they would ride to school, 'all free, gratis, and for nothing', as they would have said.'

Over to Candleford Flora Thompson

Nowadays, of course, it is not only bicycles we have to treat with care on the roads, but cars, lorries and buses — traffic which is a good deal more dangerous and fast-moving than this writer ever dreamed when she wrote this.

6 July

Today is the birthday of Beatrix Potter. Does anyone know who she was? Beatrix Potter lived quietly with her parents in a tall London house. When she was a girl, more than 100 years ago, she had an 'itch to write' and a longing to draw everything beautiful she saw. She did not find anything to write about at first (although she kept a diary in a secret code she had invented) but she drew and painted plants and animals that she saw in museums or on holiday in the country. Especially she drew her pet rabbit, hedgehogs, mice and other creatures.

One day Beatrix wanted to please a little boy she knew who was ill in bed. He was called Noel and he was five. So she wrote a story about her rabbit, drew pictures for it and sent it to him. Now she had begun, she wrote and illustrated more stories about her pets for other young friends. They enjoyed these story letters so much that they kept them carefully.

After some years it occurred to Beatrix that perhaps she could make a book for children. She found that Noel had kept 'The Tale of Peter Rabbit' and she made it a little longer and offered it to publishers. But six of them, one after the other, said 'No, thank you'.

But Beatrix didn't give up. She took her savings out of the bank and paid to have copies of 'Peter Rabbit' printed, choosing small-size pages with a picture on every other one. There was one coloured picture and the rest were black and white. She found it easy to sell copies of the book to her friends. When one of the publishers saw it, he said that if she would make all the illustrations into coloured ones he would like to publish the book after all. And so 'Peter Rabbit' came to be sold in all the bookshops and was a great success. That was in 1900, [86] years ago. Since then the same

publisher, Frederick Warne, has published millions of copies of Beatrix Potter books and they have been translated into 13 different languages. And thousands and thousands of children, and their grandchildren and great grand children have enjoyed the stories of Peter Rabbit, Benjamin Bunny, Squirrel Nutkin, Mrs Tiggy Winkle, Hunca Munca, Mr Jeremy Fisher and all the rest of the little Beatrix Potter books.

A life of labour

'Work — work — work!
My labour never flags;
And what are its wages? A bed of straw,
A crust of bread – and rags.
That shatter'd roof, – and this naked floor –
A table – a broken chair –
And a wall so blank my shadow I thank
For sometimes falling there!

Work — work — work,
In the dull December light,
And work — work — work,
When the weather is warm and bright –'

The song of the shirt Thomas Hood

Imagine a life like this. From the moment you wake in the morning until late at night, thirteen or fourteen hours of continual work.

If you had been born a hundred years ago, this might well have been *your* life, now, at the age you are at this moment.

There were very large numbers of young children employed in the mines and factories of Britain. Children opened and closed the trapdoors in the coalmines. They hauled coal up steep slopes and ladders, on their backs or in heavy wagons.

July

They crawled under machines in textile factories to sweep up waste material, risking their lives and their limbs every time they did so. They climbed into chimneys to clean them out. In fact they did any kind of work that did not need special knowledge or skills.

Many started work at the age of six, working from five o' clock in the morning sometimes until eight or nine at night. Within a few years their bodies were hopelessly twisted from the hard labour and long hours. One boy described how 'in the morning I could scarcely walk, and my brother and sister used out of kindness to take me under each arm, and run with me to the mill, and my legs dragged on the ground. In consequence of the pain I could not walk.'

These horrors were treated as unfortunate, but things which had to happen in order to keep the country's industry running! Children were very cheap to employ, their wages were so small.

At the same time, there were people who worked very hard, for a great many years, to stop child labour in factories, mills and mines. One was Lord Shaftesbury, a Member of Parliament who worked until the end of his life to improve working conditions, and who was particularly concerned with helping the thousands of British children condemned to this misery.

The first blow against child labour was struck in July of 1833. A new law was passed that said no child under nine could work in cotton, wool or flax mills. No child under thirteen could work for more than nine hours a day; and no one under eighteen for more than twelve hours a day.

It did not apply to other kinds of factories, nor to the mines. It was another ten years or so before that happened. But it was nevertheless a very important beginning in the battle to outlaw child labour.

9 July
Aborigine Day in Australia. ▶ MCF.

14 July
Bastille Day in France. ▶ MCF.

19 July
The *Mary Rose* sank in 1545. *See* October 12th.

21 July
Does anyone know what happened [17] years ago today? It was at 2.56 in the morning on July 21st, 1969, that the first man stood on the moon. Neil Armstrong in his bulky protective suit inched his way slowly down the ladder of the lunar bug, Eagle, and stepped on to the surface of the moon. 'That's one small step for a man', he said 'one giant leap for mankind.'

Ever since people have been on earth, they have gazed up at the distant moon and wondered what it was like up there. And now, thanks to television cameras, some 600,000,000 people watching and listening all round the world were able to see a man walk on the moon. What *was* it like? The astronauts described a fairly level plain covered with craters of two metres wide with some ridges of rock – and thousands of little craters of half a metre or less. There were angular blocks of rock about a metre in size. And everywhere it was grey, all grey – a light chalky grey as they looked towards the sun and a darker grey as they looked away from the sun.

'Although the surface appears to be very finely grained', said Armstrong, 'As you get close to it, it is almost like a powder . . . I can pick it up loosely with my toe. It adheres in fine layers like powdered charcoal to the sole and sides of my boots . . . I can see the footprints of my boots and the treads in the fine sandy particles.'

Those footprints left by the astronauts will still be there today – undisturbed in the stillness of the moon.

Armstrong and Aldrin walked on the moon for about two and a quarter hours – setting up equipment which would be left there to send signals back to earth, taking photographs and collecting samples of soil and rock. Then they returned to the lunar module to go back to the command module and so, safely, back to earth.

Behind them, they left not only their footprints and equipment that was too heavy to take back, but also medals of five Russian and American astronauts (four of whom had died in space attempts), messages from the leaders of 70 different countries and a plaque which said:

> HERE
> MEN FROM THE PLANET EARTH
>
> FIRST SET FOOT
> UPON THE MOON
> JULY 1969 AD
>
> WE CAME IN PEACE FOR ALL MANKIND

Although it is Armstrong and Aldrin who have their names in the history books they were, in fact, only one very small part of the huge effort that made the landing possible. There were the other astronauts who had trained just as hard but who had not been chosen for the trip; there was Collins who orbited alone in the command module waiting while they made the historic descent; there were all the people in mission control at Houston who directed the flight and the thousands and thousands of people who had worked on the project: scientists, engineers, technicians, doctors, mechanics and every sort of worker. People who built the space craft, trained the astronauts, made and tested the equipment, did the paperwork and all the small boring jobs that keep things running smoothly.

When we think about great occasions like these, we should remember all the people whose names are not recorded, who get none of the glory, the fame or the excitement but whose skill and patient, hard work in the background make it all possible. *See also* Class Assembly on space, page 118.

22 July

In 1911 at this time of year Robert Scott's expedition to reach the South Pole was well underway. In the Antarctic it is winter just now. What was it like living through one of those terrible winters in that great region of ice and snow?

Here is an entry from the diary of one member of the expedition, Apsley Cherry-Garrard. He and his two companions are trapped in a blizzard a long way from their winter quarters. They are cold, weak and exhausted. As shelter, they have built an igloo from blocks of ice and rocks, using a sledge covered with canvas as the roof. Outside they pitch their tent, containing all their equipment.

'But already we had been out twice as long in winter as the longest previous journeys in spring. The men who made those journeys had daylight where we had darkness, they had never had such low temperatures, generally nothing approaching them, and they had seldom worked in such difficult country. The nearest approach to healthy sleep we had had for nearly a month was when during blizzards the temperature allowed the warmth of our bodies to thaw some of the ice in our clothing and sleeping-bags into water. The wear and tear on our minds was very great. We were certainly weaker. We had a little more than a tin of oil to get back on, and we knew the conditions we had to face on that journey across the Barrier; even with fresh men and fresh gear it had been almost unendurable.'

270 metres up a mountain slope, they scramble into the igloo, thaw out their sleeping-bags, and try to get some sleep. During the night, their tent is blown away and their equipment scattered far and wide. Snow drifts through the cracks in the igloo walls, even though they plug the holes with cloth-

ing. Then the roof of the igloo rips to shreds. With no shelter, they cannot survive. Without the tent for the return journey, there is no question of ever reaching base again.

There is only one thing to do – to try to survive the blizzard in their sleeping-bags, and then try to find the tent.

Singing songs to keep their spirits up, they wait . . .

'It was in the early morning of Saturday (July 22) that we discovered the loss of the tent. Some time during that morning we had had our last meal. The roof went about noon on Sunday and we had had no meal in the interval because our supply of oil was so low; nor could we move out of our bags except as a last necessity. By Sunday night we had been without a meal for some thirty-six hours.

The rocks which fell upon us when the roof went did no damage, and though we could not get out of our bags to move them, we could fit ourselves into them without difficulty. More serious was the drift which began to pile up all round and over us. It helped to keep us warm of course, but at the same time in these comparatively high temperatures it saturated our bags even worse than they were before . . .

Meanwhile we had to wait. It was nearly 70 miles home and it had taken us the best part of three weeks to come. In our less miserable moments we tried to think out ways of getting back, but I do not remember very much about that time. Sunday morning faded into Sunday afternoon – into Sunday night – into Monday morning. Till then the blizzard had raged with monstrous fury; the winds of the world were there, and they had all gone mad . . . I wondered why it did not carry away the earth.

In the early hours of Monday there was an occa-

July

sional hint of a lull . . . Seven or eight more hours passed, and though it was still blowing we could make ourselves heard to one another without great difficulty. It was two days and two nights since we had had a meal.

We decided to get out of our bags and make a search for the tent. We did so, bitterly cold and utterly miserable, though I do not think any of us showed it. In the darkness we could see very little, and no trace whatever of the tent. We returned against the wind, nursing our faces and hands, and settled that we must try and cook a meal somehow. We managed about the weirdest meal eaten north or south. We got the floor-cloth wedged under our bags, then got into our bags and drew the floor-cloth over our heads. Between us we got the primus alight somehow, and by hand we balanced the cooker on the top of it . . . The flame flickered in the draughts. Very slowly the snow in the cooker melted, we threw in a plentiful supply of pemmican, and the smell of it was better than anything on earth. In time we got both tea and pemmican, which was full of hairs from our bags, penguin feathers, dirt and debris, but delicious. The blubber left in the cooker got burnt and gave the tea a burnt taste. None of us ever forgot that meal; I enjoyed it as much as such a meal could be enjoyed, and that burnt taste will always bring back the memory.

It was still dark and we lay down in our bags again, but soon a little glow of light began to come up, and we turned out to have a further search for the tent. Birdie went off before Bill and me. Clumsily I dragged my eider-down out of my bag on my feet, all sopping wet; it was impossible to get it back and I let it freeze; it was soon just like a rock. The sky to the south was as black and sinister as it could possibly be. It looked as though the blizzard would be on us again at any moment.

I followed Bill down the slope. We could find nothing. But, as we searched, we heard a shout somewhere below and to the right. We got on a slope, slipped, and went sliding down quite unable to stop ourselves, and came upon Birdie with the tent, the outer lining still on the bamboos. Our lives had been taken away and given back to us. We were so thankful we said nothing.'

The Worst Journey in the World Apsley Cherry-Garrard
See also December 14th.

27 July

There is a traditional belief that on this day of the Great Flood, Noah sent a dove from the Ark to see if dry land had appeared.

The story of the flood told near the beginning of the Bible is not the only tale of this kind. For thousands of years, people all over the world have told stories like this. In some the flood is a punishment from a god, angry with people's evil ways. In others, the flood just happens, and then God steps in when it is over and helps the survivors start their lives anew.

This story is from an island in Indonesia.

There came a time when the sea rose up and flooded the whole earth. Men, women, children, animals, birds, plants, trees – everything was drowned. Even the highest mountains were swallowed – every one, that is, except the highest peak of all, the Mount of Lakimola.

A family had clambered there, taking a few animals up the craggy slopes with them. And there they waited. The days went by. Each hour the waters crept a little higher. Each hour the land on which they stood became a little smaller. Until at last it was so small that they were certain their last hour was near.

'Oh sea,' they prayed. 'Don't swallow us! Return to your old bed.'

The sea heard their plea. It said (thinking it would be too clever for them), 'I will not swallow you if you can show me an animal who has too many hairs for me to count.'

They showed a pig. The sea could quite easily count the hairs on that animal's skin! It crept a little closer to the family's feet. They showed a goat. But this, too, was well within the powers of the sea.

In vain they showed a dog and then a hen. The sea had no trouble counting both of them. By now it was lapping coldly at the family's ankles.

At last they showed a cat. The sea stared at the thick, gleaming coat, and knew at once it had been beaten. That many hairs it could not possibly count! It stopped, and rose no more.

At once a great sea-eagle appeared, and from high in the sky, it sprinkled earth across the surface of the waters. Now the family could come down from Lakimola's peaks onto dry, flat land.

God said to the sea-eagle, 'Bring seeds. Bring maize, millet, rice and beans, and sesame.'

And he said to the family, 'Sow them, and you will have food. Have children, and your children will spread over the whole earth. Once more there will be people living in every land.'

The little family looked up at Lakimola rising high above them, and gave hearty thanks to the great peak for having saved their lives.

And every year since then, the people who live below the peaks of Lakimola also give thanks that their ancestors were saved so long ago.

See also September page 12, April page 80. Class Assembly page 123.

Earthquake

In July 1984 there was the largest recorded earth tremor in parts of Britain for 20 years. But

these things don't happen very often in this country.

It is difficult to imagine what it must be like to live with the knowledge that a big earthquake may hit your home, or where tremors happen so often that you get quite used to it.

Here is a story about three children, one hot July in Jamaica. They have made friends with a wandering Rastafarian preacher, Marcus, and together they are exploring the hillsides, searching for cracks in the earth caused by the small tremors which they have been noticing for several days . . .

'Polly was standing over her brothers and staring at the cracks. Just as she was about to kneel beside Doug, a shifting, twisting tremor shook the clearing, and the rumble began again. In a fraction of a second, the high banking of the incline on which Marcus was leaning sagged, disintegrated rapidly, and crashed down on top of him.

Polly screamed. Ricky and Doug gasped in horror . . .

They shuddered. Their legs felt weak. Their mouths were dry. The palms of their hands became clammy. And their skin tightened all over. Everything went dead inside them and the outside world ceased temporarily to exist: the entire Sunday afternoon, the noise that had accompanied the landslide, the gasping horror and the scream all seemed a million miles away, encased in a capsule of silence. It was as if the whole thing had happened in a waking dream, in another country, in another time, and to *other* people.

Ricky, Doug and Polly stood and stared at the enormous mound of earth that had buried Marcus. They stood there panic-stricken, frozen . . .

Slowly, the desolate figures moved towards the mound, inching their way across the cracks in the clearing and scuffing the chipped stones and clods of earth that had come down with the landslide . . .

'Marcus is dead.' Polly was the first to speak . . .

'Maybe he's only covered over,' Doug said.

'He's dead,' Polly whispered.

'Covered over, Polly,' Doug insisted, partly to soothe her and partly to convince himself that it was so.

'*Covered over,*' Ricky repeated, and instantly the meaning of the words became clear. 'That's it,' he said, 'that's it, we'll dig him out.'

They sprang forward and pounced on the mound with their fingers curved like claws and their arms swinging like flails. They tore at the earth and scooped it up in frenzied fistfuls. Their hands worked at a terrific speed, biting into the bulk of the mound and reducing it, second after second, like a team of inspired treasure hunters certain of their trove.

They were working against time. Marcus had been buried under the landslide about a minute and a half, maybe a little longer, time enough for him to have been suffocated by the heat and the weight of the earth. But they no longer thought about that. They couldn't. They had to save him. *Marcus had to be rescued*

After they had dug for about thirty seconds, the first thing they came to was Marcus's bundle. Doug pulled the stick out of the tight dirt-filled knot and drove it deep into the scar of the excavation: then he prodded the spot to see if he could locate the general direction in which Marcus's body lay hidden . . .

Doug was the first to make contact as he swiftly got through to Marcus's left leg. When he lifted it and let it go, it dropped back lifelessly into the dirt. Ricky and Polly saw what happened and they were affected by it, but they kept on digging. Soon afterwards, Polly cleared Marcus's thigh and waist. Then Ricky reached his head. And after a few vigorous wiping strokes from Doug, the length of the left side of the body was revealed. Marcus was lying on his stomach, with his face resting in the wide V of his open Bible. As a result, the lower part of his face, his nose, mouth and chin, hadn't a trace of dirt on it.

He was breathing.

Earthquake Andrew Salkey

Marcus recovers. No one else is hurt, and life returns to normal, much as it was before the tremors began. The children have pleasure in remembering that their quick-thinking saved their friend's life.

We are fortunate nowadays that scientists have developed ways of forecasting which way earthquake shocks will travel, so that people can be warned, and if possible leave an area where a serious earthquake is likely to happen.

See also November 1st.

NEGROES

for Sale
A negro woman,
twenty-four years of age and her two children,
one eight and the other three years old.
Said negroes would be sold

separately

or together, as desired.
The woman is a good seamstress.
She will be sold low for cash, or exchanged for groceries.

This advertisement appeared in an American newspaper, *New Orleans Bee* during the last century.

(The word 'negroes' is the word that was used at that time for African people.) Advertisements like this were commonplace. For, over a period of 350 years (1520 to 1870), nearly 10 million Africans – men, women and children – were ripped from their homes in Africa and shipped across the Atlantic Ocean to serve as slaves in the plantations of North and South America and the West Indian islands.

Goods made in the workshops of Europe were taken by ship to the part of the west coast of Africa then known as the Slave Coast. They were exchanged for people who had been captured in the interior of the continent, and brought to the coast chained together. Branded, imprisoned in the trading forts dotted all along the coast, these people were known as 'black ivory' because of the vast amounts of money they were worth when sold.

Then they were loaded onto slaveships. As many as a quarter died before they reached the other side of the Atlantic. Here is a description of a slaveship, written at the time.

'The ship had taken in 336 males and 226 females on the coast of Africa, making in all 562 and had been out seventeen days during which she had thrown overboard 55. The slaves were all enclosed under grated hatchways between decks. The space was so low that they sat between each other's legs, and stowed so close together that there was no possibility of their lying down or at all changing their position night or day. Over the hatchway stood a ferocious-looking fellow with a scourge of many twisted thongs in his hand, who was the slave-driver of the ship . . .'

In the Americas, the slaves were exchanged for goods such as sugar, tea, coffee, cotton, tobacco, and indigo (used for making dyes). The ships took these goods back and sold them for a large profit in Europe.

For the slaves left behind, there was nothing but a lifetime of hard labour on the plantations.

Here is what one slave wrote of his experiences.

'An hour before daylight the horn is blown. Then the slaves arouse, prepare their breakfast, fill a gourd with water, in another deposit their dinner of cold bacon and corn cake, and hurry to the field again. It is an offense invariably followed by a flogging to be found at the quarters after daybreak. Then the fears and labours of another day begin and until the close there is no such thing as rest . . .

. . . with the exception of ten or fifteen minutes, which is given to them at noon to swallow their allowance of cold bacon, they are not permitted to be a moment idle until it is too dark to see, and when the moon is full, they often times labour till the middle of the night.'

Twelve years a slave Solomon Northup

While there were many people who made a lot of money from slave-labour, there were also people who wanted to see slavery at an end. People like Granville Sharp, Olaudah Equiano and William Wilberforce formed anti-slavery societies, worked in Parliament, and gathered information and travelled the country showing people all the horrors of what was being done to slaves.

They had a hard battle because many powerful people wanted the slave trade to continue because they were making so much money from it. However, in 1807 the anti-slavers had their first success, when a law was passed forbidding people to buy and sell slaves in the countries which Britain ruled. But the slave trade went on *illegally* for another fifty years.

And of course it was still legal to own a slave. So the next thing to do was free the slaves themselves.

At the end of this month in 1833, Britain freed all the slaves on British plantations. Over the next 20 years, many other countries did the same. But there were also many who didn't, so slavery continued to exist for quite a long time. It is quite a shock to realise that it didn't really stop until the 1880s – that is, only about 100 years ago!

28 July
Hans Andersen died in 1875. *See* April 2nd.

29 July
Saint Olaf's Day in Norway, the feast day of the country's patron saint. ▶ MCF.

30 July
About forty years ago today in 1947 a small group of men floating on a log raft in the Pacific Ocean sighted a Polynesian island. It was the first land they had seen for three months.

There was great excitement. Not only was their journey nearly at an end, but they had proved what they had set out to prove. It *was* possible to cross the Pacific Ocean from South America to the Polynesian islands on the kinds of seacraft that would have been used nearly 1500 years ago.

The raft and the men on it were the Kon-Tiki expedition. The leader, a Norwegian named Thor Heyerdahl, was convinced that a tall white people who had settled in Polynesia about CE 500 had come from the west coast of South America. They had obviously crossed the Pacific Ocean to do so.

The ancient Incas of Peru in South America told of a white king called Kon-Tiki who had sailed across the sea to the west. On the other side of the Pacific, the Polynesians told stories of a white god called Tiki who had arrived there from across the seas to the east. Thor Heyerdahl was convinced that Tiki and Kon-Tiki was the same person. But many experts thought this idea was nonsense, mainly because they did not believe that people could have sailed so far in those days.

Heyerdahl decided to prove it could be done. He and his companions built a raft exactly as Kon-Tiki would have done all that time ago. It was made from great logs of balsa wood – lighter than cork when it is dry. It grows in the forests of Peru. They made the deck with split bamboo canes, covered with loose mats of plaited bamboo reeds. On top was a small cabin, also built from bamboo, and thatched with banana leaves. A canvas sail and a mango-wood steering oar completed their home for the next ninety-three days.

On 30th July 1947 they reached Polynesia. In fact they were unable to land because of winds and currents in the sea. In the end, they ran onto a coral reef and were nearly drowned.

But they survived. And in later years, Heyerdahl also crossed the Atlantic in a boat made from reed papyrus, just like the ones the Ancient Egyptians would have used.

Thor Heyerdahl had two kinds of courage: firstly, he went on believing in his ideas when other people laughed at him, and secondly, he set forth on vast and stormy oceans in tiny, primitive craft.

Leavers' song

Words and music by
Jan Holdstock

All: *End of the term,*
    End of the year,
    It's time to say
    Goodbye, Goodbye, Goodbye.

1 **Stayers:**
    You are moving on,
    Next year you'll be gone.
    We'll miss you, you've helped us so,
    We don't want to see you go.
    End of the term, etc.

2 **Leavers:**
    It's so hard to go
    Leaving friends that we know.
    Thank you for happy days,
    We'll remember this school always.
    End of the term, etc.

3 **Stayers:**
    You aren't going far
    Come and tell us how you are.
    Good luck in all you do,
    Our good wishes go with you.

    All: *End of the term,* etc.

▶ECUS Nos 54, 55

Introduction

An alternative to the teacher-dominated assembly is one produced by the children themselves. These days more and more schools are including class assemblies in their rota of services. They add variety to the act of worship and give the children a chance to show what they can do. They also provide a good opportunity for small groups of parents to share more fully in the day-to-day life of the school.

The child-based assembly encourages boys and girls to think about the material and its relevance, use their developing creative skills, practise the arts of selection and discrimination, and to work together as a team. Once a class has tried producing an assembly, they become a more sympathetic and appreciative audience for assemblies presented by other classes.

There are pitfalls as well, of course. There always are where young children are concerned! It is not always easy to find suitable material. It is sometimes difficult to ensure that all the children in the class contribute fully to the limits of their capabilities. The organisation and execution of a class assembly can become confused and anarchic, leading the teacher to take a more prominent part than was envisaged.

However, those of us who have used class-based assemblies regularly in our schools know that, with a modicum of goodwill and a certain amount of flexibility, most obstacles may be overcome, and that the results more than make up for the effort involved.

The examples of class assemblies given in this section should help any teacher to get started. The ideas come from teachers from all over the country and are extremely varied, but they all have one thing in common: they bear the hall-mark of practical use. These assemblies have been tried and tested in schools; they are so realistic that we can almost smell the wet wellies and hear the caretaker grumbling in the corridor outside.

The ways in which class services are used will depend upon individual circumstances. Some teachers will prefer, at least in the early stages, to keep a close check on what is going on. Others will give the children their heads and will not edit the results until later.

One method I have found useful in helping children to organise their own services is to compile a series of Assembly Cards. Over a period of time these can be prepared by the children themselves. On a series of stiff cards they can gradually assemble a collection of brief stories, biographies, poems, songs and prayers on a number of themes. When the time comes to put an assembly together these cards may be consulted and utilised.

Whatever approach is chosen, teachers who become involved in class assemblies will find the process stimulating and well worth the effort. There are few better ways of really getting to know the children in the class!
Graeme Kent

Contents

First Day at School

A millionbillion willion miles from home
Waiting for the bell to go. (To go where?)
Why are they all so big, other children?
So noisy? So much at home they
must have been born in uniform
Lived all their lives in playgrounds
Spent the years inventing games
that don't let me in. Games
that are rough, that swallow you up.

And the railings.
All around, the railings.
Are they to keep out wolves and monsters?
Things that carry off and eat children?
Things you don't take sweets from?
Perhaps they're to stop us getting out
Running away from the lessins. Lessin.
What does a lessin look like?
Sounds small and slimy.
They keep them in glassrooms.
Whole rooms made of glass. Imagine.

I wish I could remember my name
Mummy said it would come in useful.
Like wellies. When there's puddles.
Lellowwellies. I wish she was here.
I think my name is sewn on somewhere
Perhaps the teacher will read it for me.
Tea-cher. The one who makes the tea.

Roger McGough

At the beginning of the school year, I like to plan an assembly with older children to welcome new children to the school. In class we read Roger McGough's poem 'First Day at School' (see above) and then we talk about our memories of first days at school. Then everyone writes about these memories.

For the assembly we choose the smallest children in the class to act the 'new ones'. They sit in front of a painting of railings (on frieze paper) with the other larger children standing on a different level behind the railings.

The largest child introduces the assembly, welcoming the new children and reminding everyone in the school of what it felt like to be new by introducing one or two of the children's essays or points spoken by the larger children.

The smaller 'new' children then start saying the McGough poem. They say the first two lines of the first verse as a chorus, (likewise in the second verse), then speak a line or two in turn – turning to each other with their questions. As they speak, the bigger children look down on them, point and maybe make comments – related to the words of the poem (Aren't they little . . .? 'Look at that one over there . . .' 'You know you're not allowed to . . .') I try to help the children to get the contrast between the shyness and bewilderment of the 'new' children and the confidence of the 'older' ones.

We finish with more first-day memories and a repeated welcome and the assurance to the new children that they can rely on everyone to help them and make them feel at home.

Final prayers written and read by the children mention ways in which everyone can be kind and helpful to the new children – perhaps with a response from the rest of the school 'Please God help us to remember . . .' or something suggested by the children.

Angie Butler

St Luke's Day – October 18th

I happened to be doing a first aid course at this time of year, and as St Luke was a doctor it seemed a good idea to have a medical/first aid assembly on St Luke's Day.

We started with a highly dramatic 'operation' to get everyone's attention. A prostrate patient suffered the ministrations of a team of surgeons armed with a variety of lethal-looking instruments. Stuffed tights, tied at intervals, were extracted and the patient was stitched up with a vast cardboard needle and pronounced cured. After that, different groups mimed home nursing situations: making a patient comfortable, taking a pulse, giving medicine (shaking the bottle, putting it out of reach of small children) with a commentary by a narrator. Then other groups mimed emergency situations: nose bleed, a burn, fainting, profuse bleeding . . . while the narrator described the correct treatment that was being administered.

Finally we told the story of Florence Nightingale and sang 'Kum by ah'.

This was a very popular assembly, with a lot of children afterwards wanting to talk about their own illnesses and operations. Now we have first aid assemblies at regular intervals – I try to include a touch of humour and the dramatised form is a good way to remind children of the procedures for emergencies.
Mollie Sumsion

Warning Lights

This assembly was one of six different assemblies on the subject of light prepared by six different classes in the weeks leading up to Christmas. One class chose to look at light as a warning of danger.

Lighthouses were an obvious example of this but when the children searched the books in the class and school library they found that lights were used at sea in other ways to warn of hazards and dangers.

A model lighthouse was built with pâpier maché round a cardboard tube and a bulb holder was fixed at the top so that the light could flash. Several paintings and diagrams were made to show the different arrangements of red, green and white lights which ships use at night when moving, on tow or at anchor.

The assembly began with the hymn 'Morning has Broken'. Then one of the boys read his piece explaining how light was used by sailors to warn of danger. Other children held up their pictures of ships with different arrangements of lights and explained their significance. The model lighthouse was produced and a girl told the audience why lighthouses were so important. She explained why they flashed instead of shining steadily.

Then the story of Grace Darling was told while some of the children mimed the action. The shipwrecked sailors enjoyed waving their arms in distress and supplication, and Grace and her father rowed through the stormy seas to save them.

Finally, a short prayer composed by the children was said thanking God for the gift of light and asking him to help all lighthouse keepers to do their work well.

The assembly ended with the hymn 'Jesus Bids Me Shine with a Pure Clear Light'.
D William Blades

Teacher Witches at Hallowe'en

The basic idea of this assembly was that teachers are like witches – weaving spells to make children into kind and clever people.

We started and finished the assembly with 'Witch Song' by Grace Meserve (from *Music for Pleasure, Music for Fun*,) with glockenspiel accompaniment.

Children dressed as witches sat on stools holding large spell books. There was a large cauldron in the middle of the stage. The witches recited:

'The witch glared at her spell books
then looked up with a sigh,
What shall I do with thirty kids
now Hallowe'en is nigh?

Last year we made turnip lanterns
and played bob-apple too,
We've made ginger men and witches' hats
now what can I do?

The witch in this poem is a teacher and this assembly tells what our teacher decided to do.

Witch Walton watches
Stirs the brew,
Ear of Aaron, Duncan's shoe,
Susan's eyelash, Simon's chin,
Jonathan's knee-cap
Come stir them in.

Batty Butler comes to watch
Throws in two of Heidi's socks,
Singing, cackling, full of glee,
Talana's toes and Nina's knee.
All go in to make the spell
Natasha's nose goes in as well.

Next comes Stuart's two front teeth
From those sun-flowers pluck a leaf.
Bubbling boiling, Margaret's finger
Class Five is not a place to linger.
Ryan, Beth and Andrew, too,
None escape the boiling brew.

Tongue of Scott and Karen's lips
And Melanie from where she sits,
Beta Books and S.R.A.
These wicked crones will have their way.
Louise and Neil and Russell shake
Helen and Sam an arm they take.

Nothing escapes, no-one, no thing
Nicola, Alison, Paula's ring
Debbie, Bethia, Jonathon
It's one for all and all for one,
Even Tracy, sweet young thing,
Is lured beneath the old bat's wing.

All are mixed and churned about
At the end of term what will come out?
Happy faces, helpful too,
Children we'll be proud of you!
Clever people that's our wish,
Our charms and spells
Help make the dish.'

(The names in the poem can be altered to fit any class.) As each child's name was mentioned a piece of clothing or large cardboard body part was handed to the witches by cats and tossed into the cauldron. (Each child could put in its own.)

After the poem, the children discussed the things they'd learned since they first came to school and decided that it was a bit like magic and the teacher witches had done quite a bit of good.

Angie Butler

Identikit Witch

Another Hallowe'en assembly included the children's own spells, witches in stories – and stories about local witches, punishments for witches etc. But the high spot of the assembly was the Identikit witch. A policeman announced:

'A figure was last seen flying over . . .'

and a basic shape on a jump stand was produced. As the description proceeded, children rushed up and added each item to the basic shape . . . black stockings . . . long black cloak . . . straggly grey hair . . . pointed black hat . . . twisted mouth . . . jagged teeth . . . green eyes . . . long nose . . . pointed shoes . . . broomstick . . . black cat.

Finally the witch stood complete. (This same technique could be used for other figures in other assemblies. Try using Blu-Tak to stick the items in place.)

David Beetlestone

Time for Assembly

This assembly arose from topic work the children had done about early ways of measuring. We had two narrators and the rest of the class were divided into four groups.

We started by looking at how people in the past measured the passage of time with the natural elements of sun, water, fire and sand. Each group in turn described the measuring devices associated with one of these and showed large pictures of them which they had drawn. We had sundials, then water clocks, then candle clocks and finally sand clocks – hour glasses and egg timers.

Then we went on to mechanical clocks and listed as many kinds of these as the children had been able to think of and each group in turn said a verse of Elizabeth Fleming's poem 'The Watchmaker's Shop',

We talked about how quickly or slowly time seems to go – depending on what you are doing. Then we suggested that people might think they spent too long in school but we would show how they didn't have time to come to school at all. (The following calculations were accompanied by children holding up large number cards and three children with minus, plus and equal cards fitting in between them to make a visual display of each new calculation.)

There are 365 days in a year. You have thirteen and a half weeks holiday in a year, which is 95 days . . . SO

365 minus 95 leaves 270 days

You sleep for nine hours each night, in one year this makes 3,285 hours which is the same as 136 days . . . SO

270 minus 136 leaves 134 days

You spend about two hours of every day eating. In one year this makes 730 hours, which is the same as 30 days . . . SO

134 minus 30 leaves 104 days

But you don't come to school on Saturdays and Sundays and with fifty two weeks in a year, that makes 104 days . . . SO

104 minus 104 leaves 0

So you don't have time to come to school at all!

Finally we said that how we tell the time is very interesting but it is not so important as how we *use* our time. Our two narrators then compared the bad and good use of time.

(Do you use it selfishly, being grumpy and moody when you can't have your own way?

OR . . . do you use your time thoughtfully, being cheerful and enjoying life? Etc.)

Finally we read the passage from Ecclesiastes about time (Chapter 3: 'A time to be born and a time to die') to soft piano accompaniment.

Jenny Raw

The Light of the World

I find a projector and slides very useful for assemblies. This one began in pitch darkness. Then one of the children recited from memory Genesis I, verses 1–5 (but it could have been tape-recorded). At the lines, '"Let there be light" and there was light' we switched on the projector with a slide of a sunlit seascape. At the end of the Genesis verses, we sang 'Thank You for Giving Us This Morning' (an alternative would be 'Morning has Broken') and showed a variety of appropriate slides on the screen. Then, while a slide of a sunset was shown, a narrator told how men used to worship the sun and made sacrifices to it and how this religion was full of terror and despair because the sun disappeared at night and seemed to die in the winter. The sun gave light to the world but man's mind was still in darkness. (We switched off the projector.)

Other speakers now joined in to tell how God had sent His son to the world and how Jesus had said 'I am the Light of the World' and here we showed a slide of Holman Hunt's picture of Jesus as the Light of the World.

We went on to say that Jesus wants us to be like Him. He said 'You are the light of the world. Men don't light a candle and put it under a jar'. We did this and everyone saw how the candle went out. 'They put it on a candlestick where it gives light to the whole house'. We lit a candle and put it in a candlestick. 'Let your light shine so before men that they may see the good things you do and praise your Father who is in heaven'.

Then we all sang 'Jesus Bids Us Shine with a Pure Clear Light' and, while it was being sung, my class lit more candles from the candle in its candlestick. (We had made candle holders from tinfoil cake cases.) So by the end of the hymn there were 30 flickering candles to light the hall.

We finished with prayers for blind people. I think mental blindness is even more in need of prayer but it was a difficult concept to grapple with so I left it for another time.

Morag Henriksen

Presents

The idea of basing an assembly on the giving of presents came from work my seven and eight-year olds were doing on love – a theme from the Cheshire R E syllabus.

The whole class helped to wrap a present in an enormous exciting-looking parcel and we put this out on a stage block in front of the rest of the school and the parents of my class. The children had decided to invite the headmaster to open the parcel. Amid mounting excitement he undid wrapping after wrapping until he arrived, knee deep in crepe paper, at his Mars bar.

Next, each of the children in turn showed their favourite presents and talked about them. Then we asked the school whether they thought the most expensive presents were best. This led some older children to say that expensive things were not always the best, and that presents could take the form of helping others or being thoughtful towards them.

Finally, we asked the parents to come in turn onto the stage to be given a surprise present. These were pendants, bracelets and medallions which the children had made from painted and varnished New Clay. We had made decorated boxes (starting by drawing nets of cubes) to hold the presents and these had been stacked in a pyramid on the stage.

To avoid hurting feelings, I explained that it was impossible for all parents to be there, however much they wanted to come, because they had to work, just as I was unable to attend my own sons' assemblies.
Hilary Walker

Christ – Born in Chadderton

We had an assembly which told the story of how St Francis first set up a crib scene at Christmas and afterwards a discussion evolved amongst the top juniors: What would happen if Mary and Joseph came to our town (Chadderton)? How would they travel? Where would they stay? How would people react to them? How would they be fed and kept warm? The children suggested that this might make the basis for a class assembly and so 'Christ – born in Chadderton' began.

The drama was worked out with the teacher fitting in the ideas suggested by the children. The play started with a scene showing Mary and Joseph in modern dress by a cardboard box with a baby in it covered in newspapers.

'What would happen if Mary and Joseph had arrived in Chadderton? Would things be any different?' asked the narrator. 'This is what we think might have happened.'

The children then acted a couple arriving at the local railway station and looking for somewhere to sleep. They visit the church, the vicarage, the pub, the 'chippy', the building site and eventually reach an old house waiting to be demolished. They are rejected by the respectable, the suspicious and those just too busy and finally it is the homeless in the derelict building who help them.

All the dialogue was made up by the children after discussion and every child in the class took part. The prayers written by the children themselves, centred on the present day unemployed and homeless. Biscuits made by the children were sold after the assembly and the proceeds sent to 'Shelter'. Music was provided by the children playing and singing modern carols.
Alan Clamp

Flight to Planet Zero

Our space assembly really started when we were given a pile of chipboard offcuts. The shape of some of these inspired us with the idea of building a space ship and, before long, we had a ship two metres tall covered in silver foil, standing outside our classroom.

This inspired a whole spate of work which culminated in our assembly.

We started with short stories the children had written about being out on space patrol and other stories about aliens orbiting unknown planets. These were accompanied by large pictures drawn by the authors. Then we revealed our spaceship and the Star Ranger Space Patrol lined up one by one and announced themselves to the school. An emergency message came from Lunar Base. A new planet had been discovered. The crew went into the Star Ranger, everyone (including the audience) counted down and the space ship was off into space. There was a commentary en route before the Star Ranger landed on the Planet Zero and an appropriate background scene was displayed. The crew emerged in their space helmets and, as they did so, described what they saw.

Then a group of Zerolings arrived (in an assortment of weird outfits and outlandish masks). One crew member tried to capture them, another tried to shoot them and others ran away screaming. Only the navigator remained. She showed herself to be friendly and so won the confidence of the aliens, and the aliens and the crew mingled together – dancing and joking.

Lunar Base broke in with the order to return and the crew went back to the spaceship. But it was out of balance and would not lift off.

The crew's efforts failed to straighten it and so the Zerolings' help was enlisted. The ship was straightened and amid farewells the countdown was given again. The ship headed for home and the school was asked to sing the class's favourite hymn ('If I were a Butterfly') and we said some prayers about friendliness.

Joe Santaniello
See also July 21st (Moon landing).

Building Bridges

We set the scene by using two forms and a gym table to construct a bridge – we covered it with sugar paper and painted a stone arch and water on it. This was used not only as a background but also for children to stand on and walk over in various dramatised items.

We started by describing different types of bridges, while a group of children illustrated the name of the different structures in movement.

For the *clapper* bridge, they made an arch and clapped hands

For the *suspension* bridge four children supported another doing a handstand

For an arch *bridge*, they did backbends . . .

. . . then turned over and revealed that they had cushions down the back of their T-shirts so that they were now *hump-backed*.

For a *flyover* bridge they leap-frogged over one child in the centre of the stage.

Next was a Mastermind sketch. Two contestants, one with the specialist subject of 'bridges', the other with the subject 'structures', answered questions. The questions and answers were devised by the children from their own work.

A child read his story about how bridges were first invented and got their name, and two stories about bridges collapsing (using train sound effects from a record) were also read. Another story about two old ladies and their favourite bridge was acted – as was a play about plans to blow up a bridge in war-time.

At this point we sang a hymn 'Everyone's Building' (*Come and Praise*, BBC).

We then explained that bridges are not only structures made out of stone and steel to link two places together, but that they can also be built between one person and another – if there is a barrier between people 'bridges' can be created to link two groups. Two stories had been written to illustrate this point and they were acted.

Finally we talked about how Jesus is our link or bridge with God and how, through prayer, we can bridge the gap between man and God and seek help in building our own 'bridges'. The children read prayers they had written asking God to help us break down the barriers between people, and other prayers about 'bridges' they needed to build – asking God for help to keep their 'bridges' strong and secure.

Fenella Phillips

Fire Fire!

In preparation for our 'Fire' assembly we studied how man uses fire, a group of children made up a shadow puppet play, others wrote about their experiences with fire – including accidents – or poems about fire and we practised playing the song 'London's Burning'.

The assembly started with a quick burst of the school fire alarm. What does it mean?

Then we looked at the history of how fire was made: flints, rubbing sticks, tinder boxes, matches, lighters – now lasers. The children talked about fires for warmth, for cooking, for protection, for celebrations and ceremonies, for signalling, for lighting and for war. They told what they had found out about the Great Fire of London, fires after the San Francisco earthquake and during the blitz. Intermixed were their own poems and experiences.

The shadow puppet play on the overhead projector (figures made of black card, flames of red cellophane) was a cautionary tale about how carelessness started a fire. The fire engines arrived and put it out.

We ended with a practical demonstration of how to dial 999 and who to ask for . . .

David Beetlestone
See also June page 95.

Many Hands . . .

The ideas for our assembly on 'Hands' multiplied until the final version lasted for an hour. It was very popular and news of it spread so that we were asked to perform it at our local comprehensive school.

We started with hand language – and the children said 'Good Morning' using their hands. Then we looked at our hands and talked about the various parts of them and compared sizes. Some children read out stories that they had written about 'A Day in the Life of a Hand' and others demonstrated hand customs: shaking hands, holding hands, hands up, salutes of various kinds, clapping hands (including games where partners clap their hands together) waving hands etc.

A group of children talked about taking our hands for granted and the problems of people with crippled hands or without hands.

Hand proverbs ('many hands make light work', 'a bird in the hand', 'the devil finds work for idle hands' etc.) were acted in brief scenes.

Max Bygrave's song 'You Need Hands' introduced a section on the skilled hands of doctors, artists, watchmakers, bricklayers, knitters, machinists, potters etc. The section concluded with an extract from Tchaikovsky's piano concerto.

'Hands for fun' was about handling pets and animals – with demonstrations with real animals. Then we had more fun with 'Hands, Knees and Boomps-a-Daisy' and dreadful puns in a TV quiz game with Handy Forsyth, Hans Handerson and Handsel Ngretel. Contestants had to give Handswers to questions about Handy Pandy, the Hand of the Baskervilles etc.

More serious information about hygiene and washing hands followed and finally we looked at religious aspects of the theme: Jesus's laying-on of hands, baptism, Jesus using his hands in the carpenter's shop and breaking the bread at the Last Supper.

Prayers written by the children and the hymn 'Hands of Jesus' concluded our marathon assembly.

Michael Johnson

Saint Patrick's Day (March 17th)

We drew a big colour picture of St Patrick, with Celtic tracery in black as background, for our assembly on March 17th. (A slide of the Book of Kells would be a good alternative.) We had a large pot of wood sorrel (elsewhere, you could, of course use real shamrock or clover). As the school came in, we played the 'credo' track from the St Patrick's Mass (RCA Stereo SF8123).

Different children told the story they had put together from their researches about Padruig, a British boy who lived on the shores of the Irish Sea near the end of Hadrian's Wall, maybe in Cumbria, maybe in Galloway.

When he was sixteen he was kidnapped by pirates and carried off to Donegal in Ireland where he was sold as a slave. (Vigorous mime accompanied this part of the story.)

After several years Padruig escaped, but he had grown to love the land of Ireland and he wanted to tell the people about Jesus Christ, to give them a religion of hope and free them from the misery and fear of their old pagan religions. So he went to Europe to train as a priest and when he was ready he came back to Ireland.

He went straight to the top, to the High King himself and, although his Druid priests tried to stop him, Padruig won in the end and the High King was baptised. (More mime.) All his life Padruig travelled about Ireland teaching and preaching about Christ. One day the King said to him, 'You say there is only one God and yet you talk about Jesus Christ as if He is the Son of God and you talk about the Holy Spirit that Jesus left behind as if He is part of God too . . . I don't understand these three Gods in one God.'

(We then displayed a large cardboard trefoil. Girl Guides may want to recognise their badge. Celtic FC supporters in Scotland do, too!) 'Here is the leaf of the shamrock – one leaf and yet three leaves in one. This plant can help us to understand God,' said Padruig. He pointed to each leaf in turn. (We turned the trefoil round to show words printed on it.)

'The Father
The Son
and the Holy Spirit,
One God but Three in One.
We call this Tri-une (3 part) God –
The Trinity.'

The King understood – and ever afterwards the shamrock has been the emblem of Ireland and Irishmen wear it on St Patrick's Day.

We then explained that St Patrick wrote many hymns in Gaelic and that the hymn we were going to sing next was a translation of one of these called 'St Patrick's Breastplate.' ('I bind unto myself this day, The strong name of the Trinity.')

Finally we said St Patrick's prayer:

Christ be with me, Christ within me,
Christ behind me, Christ before me,
Christ beside me, Christ to win me,
Christ to comfort and restore me.

Christ beneath me, Christ above me,
Christ in quiet, Christ in danger,
Christ in hearts of all that love me,
Christ in mouth of friend and stranger.

And we finished with a bit more of St Patrick's Mass.
Morag Henriksen

Liquorice Allsorts

The class prepared for this assembly by discussing how wonderfully different people are – what an amazing assortment of hair, skin, and eye colours we had, how our features, our size, our clothes were all different. Children drew their own pictures of different people.

For the assembly they had a giant collage of liquorice allsorts behind them and a box of liquorice allsorts. Children in turn pulled out an allsort from the box and described what it was like. Then they talked about how the different colours, shapes and sizes of the sweets all blend to make one box of allsorts – just as the world is made up of people of different shapes, sizes and colours.

After this the children held up their pictures and talked about the people they had painted and the teacher added her own little bit about each child – each had his or her own talents (kind or thoughtful or always smiling or full of jokes etc.)

They concluded by saying that the world is a better place because of our variations – we can all play our part. They finished by singing the 'Getting Along Together' song.
Longfield Park Community Education Centre, Coventry
See also song page 88.

Mother's Day

Before the assembly, the class talked about mothers and what they do for us and the children wrote stories and poems about their mums, painted pictures and made presents. They made some life-size paintings of mums – some of the mothers came in and lay on the floor so the children could draw round them.

They asked one of the mothers if she would come to the assembly with a washing basket and some washing and they all thought of some labels which told of the things mothers do for us:

loving, working, cleaning, shopping, nursing, cooking etc.

At the assembly they welcomed everyone and explained that this was a special washing day and then the volunteer mother came out with her washing equipment and apron. Two children held up a washing line and the mother pegged out her washing – to each garment they had pinned one of the labels. The children explained how these are some of the things that mums do – day in and day out, week in and week out, year in and year out. This was the one day when we specially remembered all that they did for us and gave thanks.

The children then displayed their paintings and others read their stories and poems. Everybody sang 'Thank You for Mothers' to the tune 'Morning Has Broken'.

Thank you for mothers

Father in heaven	Parents and children
Thank you for mothers,	Praise God together,
Loving and caring	Praise for our homes
All the day long;	And all that he gives;
Thank you for fathers,	May we serve others,
Working to feed us,	As serving Jesus
Mothers and fathers	Makes every home
Loving and strong.	The place where he lives.

Then they asked the audience if they liked secrets and they showed them a secret – a whole collection of bundles of daffodils. They explained that everyone would be able to take a daffodil home for mum, and two children from each class came up to collect a bunch of daffodils to distribute.

Longfield Park Community Education Centre, Coventry

Our Senses

This assembly is a good follow-up to work on the senses. The children chose tests that they used in classwork and devised new ones suitable for presentation at assembly. One group made recordings of different everyday sounds, another collected different objects to feel, another made up solutions of different tastes, another collected bottles and jars containing things with different smells.

The assembly started with readings from factual work and poems about our senses and then the audience was invited to try the tests. When everyone was totally quiet, the recordings were played. Who could guess what made the sounds?

Then volunteers were chosen to feel the objects in a 'feely box' and guess what they were. (If fairly large things are chosen and the back of the box is open, the audience can see the objects being felt but the volunteer, who is feeling them, can't.)

Other volunteers were given solutions to taste and things to smell while the answers were held up for the audience to read (to themselves!).

We ended by singing 'Glad that I live Am I' and with a prayer of thankfulness for our senses and the pleasures they bring us.

Mollie Sumsion

Walls and Minibeasts

The children had been investigating the insect and plant life in and around local walls and this assembly arose directly out of that work.

They started by explaining where they had been, what they had done and some of the experiments they had carried out with woodlice. Then we dramatised what they had learned about minibeasts in this way. We made two huge card boots fixed on pieces of wood which two children could move across the stage. Several other children, dressed in black bags with doodle-boppers on their heads, represented woodlice and we had a centipede and a couple of worms, too.

While the boots and the minibeasts were on the stage we had a dialogue about a professor (these were his boots) discovering the minibeasts and his observations. (This information came directly from the children's own observations and not from books.) Meanwhile there was appropriate movement of the boots and action by the minibeasts.

We acted an extract from *James and the Giant Peach* (where he enters the peach and discovers the different creatures) and read minibeast poems written in acrostic form. We also read stories that children had written after hearing the passage from 'The Secret Garden' where Mary finds the key to the garden — saying what they thought was behind the wall. Finally we played an instrumental track from Supertramp's 'Crisis What Crisis', and children dressed as spiders and flies did a mime/movement sequence of flies being caught in spiders' webs, trying to get free and the spiders appearing and devouring them.
Fenella Phillips

Superstitions

Our class assemblies take place on Fridays. Our turn came on Friday the 13th and so we had a ready-made subject.

The assembly started but was interrupted by half the class going on strike and refusing to participate because it was an unlucky day. They reluctantly agreed to continue when 'the management' assured them that someone would be touching wood throughout the performance.

The resident professor then went on to explain the meaning and the thinking behind various superstitions while groups of actors demonstrated.

a. Walking under a ladder. (A decorator spilt his paint over a careless pedestrian.)

b. Passing someone on the stairs. (Two people carrying piles of boxes or books collided on a set of stairs made from stage blocks.)

c. Spilling salt. (A diner spilt the salt and the devil appeared, to be driven off by salt thrown over the shoulder.)

d. Lighting three cigarettes from one match. (The third soldier was shot by an enemy sniper.)

After more of this kind of thing, the assembly concluded with a play telling the story of Mrs Mace and the magpies.

(We adapted the story 'Mrs Mace's Magpies' from *One World and Another – Summer* (Margaret Greaves, Methuen). The story deals with the superstitions about magpies recorded in the verse:

> One for sorrow,
> Two for mirth,
> Three for a wedding,
> Four for a birth,
> Five for silver,
> Six for gold,
> Seven for a secret
> That's never been told.

In our play, Mrs Mace wore herself out trying to keep up with these superstitions as more and more magpies appeared.)

At the very end of the assembly, as the children were congratulating themselves on having got through without any hitches, all the lights went out!
Andrew Bryden

The Story of the Flood

We are lucky because the back of our hall is separated from the dining room by removeable panels. We can take down two or three of these, hang up a sheet, put a projector behind it and we have a perfect screen for shadow plays.

This assembly, inspired by a long ago performance of Britten's *Noye's Fludde*, used the shadow screen but it could be done just as well on an open stage. We used bright costumes and simple humour like a medieval miracle play.

1 *The wickedness of the world.* While suitable music was played (Holst, The Planets: Mars) shadow actors showed gambling and theft, riots and stoning, false gods and witchcraft, torture and slavery, bloodshed and murder.

2 *Noah and his family are introduced.* They were rather puppet-like and came in like figures on a clock (Music: Kodaly – Hary Janos Suite: Musical Clock).

3 *God speaks to Noah.* While an amplified or tape-recorded voice gave the instructions for building the ark (Genesis 6, v 14–17) Noah and his sons drew plans.

4 *The ark is built.* We used verses from 'The History of the Flood' by John Heath Stubbs with accompanying actions and projected pictures on the shadow screen.

5 *The animals.* We made animal and bird masks—very big and bright and bold and the animals came on to more verses from 'The History of the Flood' animals and recorded steam fairground organ music. (But could be drawn by the children on an OHP roll and shown on the screen.)

6 *The rain starts.* A discussion between Noah and his sons about whether all the animals are on board gave us plenty of scope for jokes:

Have we got the skunks?.
(Sniffing audience) Pooh! Rather!
What about the fleas?
(Scratching) They're here somewhere.
What about the great apes?
(Points to staff) They're over there! etc.

Noah had to be reminded to take Mrs Noah and there was a struggle to get her on board.

7 *The rising flood.* We played The William Tell overture and projected a picture of the ark, gradually rocking more and more, with blue acetate waves moving up from the bottom of the screen. The children rocked to and fro on the stage and everyone sang a verse of 'Eternal Father, Strong to Save'.

8 *The ark leaks.* Dog's nose failed to stop it, so did Mrs Noah's elbow and Noah had to sit on it. (Ever since then dogs have had cold noses, women cold elbows and men have stood with their backs to the fire!)

9 *The rain ends.* The raven and the dove were acted by two children who were good at moving.

10 *The grounding of the ark.* We played Part 3 of William Tell, the ark was unloaded (more verses from 'The History of the Flood') and the animals marched off to the Royal March of the Lions from Saint Saens', Carnival of the Animals.

The OHP projected a rainbow.
Andrew Bryden
See also September page 12, April page 80, July 27th.

Slithering on Stage

One child in my class brought in a pair of slow-worms which caused so much interest that, a fortnight later, we were able to present a slow-worm assembly.

We displayed the slow-worms in an aquarium and used drapes printed with string in snake shapes as a background to the children's slow-worm sketches.

We started by reading some of the poems the children had written about slow-worms. Some of these were in the shape of slow-worms or had sketches superimposed upon them and these were taken round the audience so that they could have a closer look.

The children then displayed their sketches and prints and explained how they had been achieved and how, by looking closely at the creatures, they had noticed many interesting details.

After this, one child gave a talk about slow-worms – explaining how they were caught, looked after and so on. This was followed by a Mastermind series of questions answered by another child. The audience was then invited to ask their questions and the assembly co-ordinator chose the questioners in turn. This maintained everyone's interest and kept work at an appropriate the level.

The assembly leader then walked around displaying the creatures and some children were able to feel them for the first time. We finished with some snake-like slithering movements to the accompaniment of 'Within You, Without You' from The Beatles' 'Sergeant Pepper's Lonely Heart Club Band.'
Mary Goodsall

Loyalty and the Willow Pattern Story

Our assembly on loyalty grew from reading the story of the willow pattern plates which we found out about during a project on China. A group of good readers told the story. (A summary is given below – the full story is in *The Willow Pattern Story*, Lucienne Fontannaz, Angus and Robertson or *The Story of the Willow Pattern Plate*, A and C Black). The rest of the class mimed it, supplying occasional lines of dialogue.

We made a cardboard bridge fixed to three chairs with blue crepe paper water below and a card pagoda attached to an easel. We attached two card doves to sticks. (An alternative would have been to photograph a plate and project it as a backcloth or to use an epidiascope to project a picture of a plate – or draw a giant version ourselves.)

We used simple props and costumes: fans, pots of bamboo leaves, back-to-front pyjamas or shifts with Chinese characters on them; the flame dancers (who mimed the fire at the end of the story) had twirling red, orange and yellow streamers of crepe paper on sticks, and the soldiers wore black bin-liners with more Chinese characters painted or stuck on them.

We played a selection of music from *Ming Ming and the Lantern* (Time and Tune, Spring 1980) and used a lot of percussion and loud banging of gongs to introduce different characters.

At the end, we held up a willow pattern plate and reminded the audience that the story was about loyalty: the loyalty of Chang and Koong-Se to each other and of the maid to her mistress. We suggested that the next time they saw a willow pattern plate they should look on it to find the details of the story and remember the lesson of loyalty.

The Story

A rich mandarin's daughter, Koong-Se, falls in love with her father's poor secretary, Chang. Her father forbids them to meet, confines Koong-Se to the house and builds a wall to keep Chang away. (The mandarin's elaborate house and the wall can be seen on the plate). Koong-Se is to be married to a wealthy old nobleman, Ta-Jin. The lovers communicate with messages floated in little boats down the stream by the house. Ta-Jin arrives for the pre-wedding festivities with the gift of a box of jewels. Chang manages to get into the house in disguise and he and Koong-Se take the box of jewels and escape – her father sees them and pursues them with a whip. (On the plate there are three figures on the bridge: Koong-Se with her spindle, Chang with the jewel box and the father with his whip).

The lovers escape and take refuge with a loyal former maid of Koong-Se's. She hides them while Ta-Jin hunts for them (and his jewels). Her simple house is shown on the left of the plate. Suspicion falls on the maid and soldiers arrive and surround the house. She delays them until Chang has had time to jump into the rushing river beside the house and return with a boat to snatch Koong-Se away. (You can see the boat on the plate). The soldiers search the house but find nothing.

The lovers float down the river and build a house on an island (also shown on some plates). They live here happily for many years until one day they are tracked down by the relentless Ta-Jin. He arrives with a party of soldiers, Chang is killed and in despair, Koong-Se rushes to her apartments, sets them on fire and dies in the flames. She and Chang are transformed into two immortal doves – symbols of their love and loyalty – and these, too, appear on the plate.

Angie Butler

And so to bed . . .

Our assembly started with a reminder that we spend about a third of our lives in bed. Children then described what they had learned about beds in the past: bags of straw, benches with mattresses, 4-poster beds, Tutankamen's bed, Greek and Roman beds etc. They showed their pictures of different kinds of beds today; wooden beds, brass beds, bunk beds, air beds, water beds, folding beds, camp beds, hammocks etc. Then they read their poems about sleep. This was followed by a fashion parade of various forms of sleep wear – including a night shirt and night cap.

We looked at how people sleep in other countries – including the million people who sleep in the streets in Calcutta – and how astronauts sleep, and we finished with children's writings about 'What Mum says in the morning to get me up'.

David Beetlestone

Index

Index

Acknowledgements

Our thanks to the following people for permission to use copyright material:

Songs
Eileen Diamond for *Autumn, Autumn What Do You Bring?*

Jan Holdstock and Universal Edition (London) Ltd for *The Harvest Song*, and Jan Holdstock for *The Leavers' Song*.

Barrie Carson Turner for the words and music of *Hibernating Time*, the words and arrangement of *Pancake Tuesday* and the music for *The Wheel Around the World*.

Oxford University Press for *In Bethlehem Town* from Oxford School Music Books (Junior No 4) and *Happiness* from Oxford School Music Books (Senior No 3).

Harrap Ltd for *On a Christmas Night* from 'Singing Fun'.

Schott & Co Ltd for *Mix a Pancake* from 'Perry Merry Dixy'.

Stainer & Bell and J Tearnan and J Tillman for *The Seasons of the Year* (originally entitled *It's Autumn Once Again*).

Abingdon Press for *It's Easter*, words by Winifred E Stiles from 'Music Activities for Retarded Children', ©1965 by Abingdon Press.

Macdonald Educational for the words of *The Wheel Around the World*.

Chappell Music Ltd and International Music Publications for *Winds in Summer*.

Poems
'Haiku for Spring' from *Penguin Book of Japanese Verse* translated by Geoffrey Bownas and Anthony Thwaite, Penguin Books Ltd.

New Directions Publishing Corporation for 'A Spring Rain' from *100 More Poems from the Chinese: Love and the Turning Year* ©1970 by Kenneth Rexroth.

Philomel Books (The Putnam Publishing Group) for Eskimo Chant, 'Joy in Summer', from *Beyond the High Hills, a Book of Eskimo Poems* by Knud Rasmussen ©1961 by The World Publishing Co.

'First Day at School' from *In the Glassroom* by Roger McGough, Jonathan Cape Ltd.

Extracts from Books
Quotations from children, *New Internationalist* magazine.

The Bombard Story by Alain Bombard, Andre Deutsch (1953).

Lark Rise to Candleford and *Over to Candleford* by Flora Thompson (1954), Oxford University Press.

Walkabout by James Vance Marshall, Michael Joseph.

Julie and the Wolves by Jean Craighead George, Hamish Hamilton.

The Long Winter by Laura Ingalls Wilder, Lutterworth Press.

Avalanche by A Rutgers van der Leoff, Hodder and Stoughton.

The Ugly Duckling by Hans Christian Andersen, translated by Naomi Lewis, Penguin Books Ltd, ©Naomi Lewis (1981).

Flood Warning by Paul Berna, The Bodley Head (English translation) 1962.

The Bodhi Tree by Greta James, Geoffrey Chapman, (Cassell Ltd).

Man of Everest by James Ramsay Ullman, Harrap Ltd.

Ash Road by Ivan Southall, Angus and Robertson Ltd.

Diary of Anne Frank, Vallentine Mitchell Ltd.

Angry River by Ruskin Bond, Hamish Hamilton.

The Worst Journey in the World by A Cherry Garrard, the author's Literary Estate and Chatto and Windus.

Earthquake by Andrew Salkey, Oxford University Press (1965).

Illustrations
The Mansell Collection for pictures on pages 71, 75, 85.

Other WLE books

Music books from Ward Lock Educational

The Funny Family Alison McMorland   ISBN 0 7062 3719 6
An entertaining selection of singing games, nursery rhymes and folk songs, which will be enjoyed and treasured by young and old alike. Simple guitar chords and melody lines or piano accompaniment are provided.

Brown Bread and Butter Alison McMorland   ISBN 0 7062 4196 7
A further selection of songs, singing games and rhymes for every occasion. Many fine old favourites and captivating new discoveries have been brought together to be enjoyed wherever children play, and wherever strong local traditions still exist.

Knock at the Door Jan Betts   ISBN 0 7062 4029 4
A comprehensive collection of songs, poems and rhymes which are popular today with young children. Very simple guitar chords and melody lines are provided, and the delightful illustrations will provide many hours of enjoyment.

Sing Around Scotland Morag Henriksen and Barrie Carson Turner   ISBN 0 7062 4481 8
Morag Henriksen, a primary teacher and folk singer from the Isle of Skye, has gathered together an exciting new selection of songs from every region of Scotland. All the songs have new piano arrangements specially written by Barrie Carson Turner. Historical and geographical notes, a glossary and striking photographs complete the book.

A Musical Calendar of Festivals Barbara Cass-Beggs   ISBN 0 7062 4226 2
A collection of songs from all over the world, grouped into months with clear explanations of their appropriateness to particular festivals. The songs are beautifully illustrated and have both melody and guitar chording for accompaniment.

Barnabas the Dancing Bear Diana Holland   ISBN 0 7062 4225 4
These five plays, based on both original and well-known stories, will be greatly enjoyed by 5-8 year olds. Each play combines catchy songs with short speaking parts and offers scope for percussion work, dancing, choruses etc. All the plays are attractively illustrated.

Sing the Christmas Story Barrie Carson Turner   ISBN 0 7062 4606 3
This is a book of specially commissioned carols set within a framework of familiar readings from the Bible and offering a great range of styles, both in words and music. Each carol highlights a particlar aspect of the story: the angel's visit to Mary; the people going to be counted; the scene at the inn; the birth of the baby ... the whole sequence of events unfolds in song. Anyone planning a Christmas concert or play will find exactly what is needed in Sing the Christmas Story. The music has been carefully edited by Barrie Carson Turner to make sure that it is suitable for young singers and that the piano accompaniments can be easily played.

Alphabet Zoo Songbook Ralph McTell   ISBN 0 7062 4423 0
Here are all the favourite songs from Ralph McTell's children's television programmes — arranged for the piano for the first time. They range from the lyrical to the delightfully absurd and make the ideal basis for a school entertainment (performance suggestions are provided). Chris Masters' illustrations catch the mood of the songs perfectly. Factual details about some of the more unusual animals are included.

Sing as You Grow Brenda I. Piper   ISBN 0 7062 4158 4
The original songs in this delightful collection have been written for the very young, and are designed to encourage physical, mental, emotional and social skills. Guitar chords are included, together with suggestions for untuned percussion.

Every Colour Under the Sun   ISBN 0 7062 4266 1
Songs on thoughtful themes for primary school assemblies.
The songs in this exciting collection (many of them original) are grouped into themes: the seasons, the world around us, faith and prayer, work and everyday duties, helping others, working towards a better world, celebrations, beginnings and endings etc. Here is the answer to the teachers' need for musical material to span the range of cultures and faiths found in many schools today.

Jump into the Ring Lesley Lees   ISBN 0 7062 4294 7
A whole new treasury of original action songs and rhymes for young children. Simple piano accompaniments and guitar chords are provided plus helpful ideas for organisation and presentation. The songs, rhymes and tunes all have a strong rhythmic content, inviting and encouraging movement.

Music With Mr Plinkerton Eleanor Gamper   ISBN 0 7062 4651 9
This book, designed especially for non-specialist teachers, provides an easy-to-follow approach to teaching music to young children. Using both familiar and original songs, rhymes and activities, the book introduces concepts with the help of 'Mr Plinkerton', a colourful musical character. Packed with ideas for games and activities and containing attractive photocopiable posters, cards and pictures, Music with Mr Plinkerton provides an exciting and stimulating introduction to basic concepts such as pulse, rhythm and pitch.

Silly Aunt Sally, Jan Holdstock   ISBN 0 7062 4313 7
Have fun with your class with Silly Aunt Sally - a collection of original songs which will appeal to children's love of the ridiculous. Many of the songs have accompanying actions or games and all have fresh, catchy tunes pitched at the right level for young voices. The book contains full piano accompaniments and guitar chords for each song as well as suggestions for percussion work.

Musical Starting Points With Young Children Jean Gilbert   ISBN 0 7062 4045 6
Jean Gilbert believes that all children have musical ability, and that this can and should be developed as part of everyday activity in the classroom. The aim of this book is to help the class teacher with no specialist musical training to integrate music into the daily timetable. It describes a number of starting points, including listening, singing, percussion and exploring sound, and explains how these can be developed.

Talk About - Sing Out Brenda I. Piper   ISBN 0 7062 5193 8
A follow-up to her successful title Sing As You Grow, Talk About - Sing Out contains more of Brenda Piper's delightful original songs, designed to stimulate and encourage musical enjoyment and development in young children. Simple, catchy melodies and carefully structured lyrics promote both emotional and social awareness and pleasure in music. Each song is accompanied by suggestions for simple accompaniment and guidelines for teachers on a variety of related cross-curricular activities, practical work and discussion.